DATING

CLUES FOR THE CLUELESS

CHRISTOPHER D. HUDSON
CHRISTINE COLLARD ERICKSON
MARYANN LACKLAND
AMBER RAE
RANDY SOUTHERN
LINDA WASHINGTON
LEN WOODS

PROMISE
PRESS
An Imprint of Barbour Publishing

I0668525

Developed and produced by the Livingstone Corporation.

Interior Design by Design Corps, Batavia, IL.

Cover Design by Robyn Martins.

Cover and Interior Artwork by Elwood Smith.

ISBN: 1-57748-491-6

Published by   Promise Press, an imprint of Barbour Publishing, Inc., P.O. Box 719
                      Uhrichsville, OH 44683.

Printed in the United States of America.

 2 3 4 5 6 7 8 9 / 04 03 02 01 00

TABLE OF CONTENTS

SECTION 3

ASKING SOMEONE OUT 41

SECTION 4

ONCE YOU'VE BEEN ASKED 55

SECTION 5
THE ACTUAL DATE 71

SECTION 6
RESPECTING YOUR DATE 85

INTRODUCTION

"As soon as I get up the nerve, I'm going to ask her out."
"I'm afraid I'll clam up when I'm around him. I don't know what to say."
"Ok I've asked her out. Now what!?!?"
"Now that I've said yes, I wish I hadn't. What should I do?"
"How do I tell her that I really like her?"
"How do I know if he's the right one for me?"

Ever said one of those? You're not alone. Dating can be overwhelming and sometimes scary. There's lots of other questions, too: Am I ready to date? Who should I date? How can I ask her out? How can I make a good impression? What should I talk about with my date? How do I know when I've found the right one?

If you're like most people, your head starts spinning when you ask questions like these. There's just too much to think about, too much to worry about, and frankly, the whole idea may make you a little queezy.

Help has arrived.

No, it's not Pepto-Bismol. (But sometimes that *can* help.) Rest assured, this help is easier to swallow.

The secret is simple: know where to look. See, you don't need to have all the answers and 52 creative date ideas ready at the moment you meet Mr. or Mrs. Right. You only need to know where to find them. And this book is the place to find them. For example you'll find:

CATCH A CLUE

A Truckload of Clues. You'll learn from the success of people who have dated and survived to tell about it. You'll also learn from the failure of a few poor folks who didn't fair so well.

WIDE ANGLE

Perspective. Sometimes we get caught up in details of dating or in confusing emotions. We need help looking at the whole picture. We'll help you take a step back.

WOW!

Unbelievable Stories and Facts. Dating is one of those times in life that really generates some wild and funny stories. We've collected a few for you to enjoy.

DON'T FORGET

Important Reminders. Did you know that if you cat chicken and spinach for lunch, it's important to floss your teeth before your date? We'll give you a few reminders to help you in your quest for your next date.

THE BOTTOM LINE

The Bottom Line. We'll help you get beyond the sweaty palms and the flutters in your stomach by letting you know the most important stuff to remember.

THE BIBLE SAYS

Help from Above. Did you know that God cares about your love life? He even has a few things to say about it. You'll be surprised and often encouraged to see what He has to say.

Before you go on another date, you need to do one more thing to get ready: *read this book*. OK, well at least part of it. Feel free to read it *your* way: from cover to cover or skipping around to the parts that interest you most. No matter how you read it, you'll find it's jammed with good advice, great ideas and entertaining stories. So turn the page and keep reading. . . . Your dates will thank you!

SECTION 1

DEAL WITH YOURSELF FIRST

UNDER CONSTRUCTION

REFINING YOUR OWN CHARACTER

If most of your friends have already tested the waters of dating, chances are you're eager to go diving in after them. Singleness can be a tough thing if you're ready to date. At least, that's one way to look at it. Another way is to recognize that your single years are the last time in your life when you can legitimately focus your attention on yourself. While your friends are busy trying to build relationships, you can take some time to build and refine your own character. Here are some construction tips to get you started.

CHECK THE ORIGINAL BLUEPRINTS

The first step in refining yourself is to search out your Builder's original plans for you. To do that, you're going to need to look at the Bible. You may be surprised to learn just how much of the Bible has to do with you. That's right—*you*. If you need to know how your sexuality is wired, you can find it in Scripture. If you'd like to find out what your responsibilities are to your parents and friends, it's in the Bible. If you'd like to know a little about what the future holds for you, check God's Word. It's all in there.

To start off, though, we're recommending that you investigate what God has to say about His will for your life. Let's face it: You can plan all the refining and building projects you want, but unless they're part of God's will for your life, you're just wasting your time.

We don't want to spoil the satisfaction that comes from discovering

God's Word on your own, but we also don't want to leave you hanging. So we'll just give you a couple of references to start with, and then let you and the Holy Spirit (who will lead you) do the rest. For some interesting insight on God's will, look up the following passages:

- Numbers 14:41–45 (the consequences of disobeying God's will);
- Psalm 40:5 (excitement about what the Lord has planned); and
- Colossians 1:9–14 (praying for God's will).

CALL IN CONSULTANTS

This may be a difficult step for you, but it should ultimately prove to be pretty useful. What you're going to do is ask your parents, your siblings, your friends, and anyone else who knows you well to tell you about yourself.

Ask them to evaluate various areas of your life and tell you what they appreciate about you and what they would like to see changed in your life. Encourage them to give their honest opinions. Take notes of the negative as well as the positive things you hear from them.

During this process, guard yourself against discouragement and indignation. Don't beat yourself up over the negative responses you get. And, for heaven's sake, don't get mad at the people you recruit to help you for sharing their honest opinions! Learn to accept the bad with the good. Your goal is to find out what these people see in you and what they'd *like* to see. There's a good chance that some of your more observant friends and family members will point out potential in you that you were previously unaware of.

Don't misunderstand the purpose of this step. We are not suggesting that you change to please someone else, whether it be family members or friends. We're suggesting that you and the people you care about most take a good look at your physical, spiritual, emotional, and intellectual makeup and identify some areas to work on. Don't make the mistake of thinking that you're changing to impress someone else. Remember, your only obligations are to please the Lord first and yourself second.

START TINKERING

Based on what you learned about God's will for your life, as well as the constructive criticism of your family and friends, identify an area or two of your life that you'd like to start working on. We urge you to take it slowly, though. Don't knock down everything at once and try rebuilding yourself from scratch.

Choose an element of your personality that you'd like to work on. Let's say it's your ... hotheadedness. Tell yourself, "For the next two weeks, I am going to do everything I can not to fly off the handle when I get angry." Then, for the next two weeks, experiment with different methods of anger control. See which ones work best for you. Ask your friends and family members to chart your progress and give you feedback from time to time. See if you can develop strategies for managing and controlling your quick temper.

These refining strategies will require you to spend an inordinate amount of time thinking and worrying about yourself. That's okay (as long as it doesn't get out of hand). That's the beauty of refining your character before you get into a dating relationship. You don't have to worry about neglecting a loved one while you focus on yourself.

THE GREATEST LOVE OF ALL

DEVELOPING YOUR RELATIONSHIP WITH GOD FIRST

If it weren't for God, we wouldn't know how to love. We're not talking about the fact that He's the Creator and we wouldn't have existed without Him. That's pretty obvious. We're saying that we would have no concept of what it means to love and be loved if it weren't for the love God has shown us. Take a look at what the apostle John says on this topic:

DON'T FORGET

Why All the Fuss?

Without the love of God in us, we cannot truly love another person as He intended us to love. That's why it is so important for us to work on our relationship with God before we attempt to start a relationship with someone else.

"Dear friends, let us love one another, for love comes from God. Everyone who loves has been born of God and knows God. Whoever does not love does not know God, because God is love. This is how God showed his love among us: He sent his one and only Son into the world that we might live through him. This is love: not that we loved God, but that he loved us and sent his Son as an atoning sacrifice for our sins. Dear friends, since God so loved us, we also ought to love one another. No one has ever seen God; but if we love one another, God lives in us and his love is made complete in us." (1 John 4:7-12)

EVALUATING YOUR RELATIONSHIP WITH THE LORD

How is your relationship with God these days? Are you inseparable? Do you stay in fairly regular contact? Do you get together every other weekend or so? Do you feel like you're drifting apart?

There's a wise old saying that goes, "If you feel distant from God, guess which one of you moved."

We can blame many things for disrupting our relationship with the Lord—busy schedules, personal problems, the fast pace of our lives. But the reasons for the disruption aren't really the point, are they? The point is solutions. It's very important that we maintain a close relationship with the Lord. Only by staying near Him can we know what He has in mind for us and our relationships.

Do you doubt that God is interested in something as trivial as our dating relationships? Think again. In Matthew 10:29-31, Jesus explains that His heavenly Father is aware of every time a sparrow falls to the ground. If He knows that much about birds, Jesus argues, how much more does He know and care about human beings, who were made in His image?

STRENGTHENING YOUR RELATIONSHIP WITH THE LORD

Recognizing that you're not as close to God as you should be is the first step in correcting the situation. The second step is to sit down with Him for a nice, long conversation about what's been going on. Talk to God about the things in your life that have been keeping you from Him. Ask for His forgiveness; then ask Him to help you remove those obstacles from your life. Tell him how you're feeling about the people and situations in your life. Ask Him for His guidance and direction as you start to date. Ask Him to give you the wisdom to recognize the people He would have you date.

And then listen.

Prayer, you see, is a two-way conversation. You talk to God, and God talks to you. You won't hear His voice, but you'll get a sense of His presence. And if you're able to block out the distractions around you, you may understand His words deep within your soul.

If you're interested in discovering God's will for your life—including for your dating relationships—crack open the Bible. Where should you start? Why not look at one of the most complete definitions of love found anywhere: 1 Corinthians 13? After that, you can check out what God's Word says about sexual intimacy in Proverbs 5:15–19 (look past the literary imagery and you'll find that the passage is describing the physical relationship between a husband and wife) and 1 Corinthians 6:18–7:9.

Don't make the mistake of thinking that God's Word is outdated and has nothing to say to us today. The Lord gave us the Bible to communicate clearly to people of every generation what lies in store for us if we commit ourselves to Him.

ONE STEP AT A TIME

LEARNING TO BE A FRIEND

What do you call a male acquaintance who spends much of his time in the company of a specific female, romancing her and laying the groundwork for a possible future together? You call him a boyfriend. And what do you call a member of the female gender whose thoughts and priorities generally center on one particular male human being? You call her a girlfriend.

Take a look at the similarities in the names of these two people. Boy*friend.* Girl*friend.* Hmm. That would seem to suggest that if you want to have a romantic relationship with someone, you're going to have to be a *friend.* It would also seem to suggest that until you've learned to be a good friend, you're not going to be a good boyfriend or girlfriend.

But what does it mean to be a good friend? Let's take a look at some of the characteristics that make up a *bueno amigo.*

A good friend is someone who can be depended upon.

A good friend always has a shoulder ready when it's needed to cry on. A good friend is ready with a listening ear when there's sharing to be done. A good friend can be counted on for just about anything. No inconvenience is too great and no problem is too small for a good friend. A good friend isn't afraid to put himself in a position to be taken advantage of. A good friend can (but never should) be taken for granted. You can always assume that a good friend will be there for you.

A good friend is someone who can be confided to.

A good friend will keep all of your secrets, except the ones that could hurt you. A good friend has no interest in gossiping to others about the things you share. A good friend will not use your words against you under any circumstances. When you open up to a good friend, you can be confident that no one else will ever hear what you say.

Start Close to Home

WIDE ANGLE

How well do you measure up in the friend department? In what areas are you strong? In what areas are you lacking? What do you need to do in order to become an even better friend? Only after you tackle these questions can you start thinking about being a good boyfriend or girlfriend.

A good friend is someone who can speak the truth in love.

A good friend will listen to everything you have to say, but will not automatically agree with you. A good friend cares enough about you and is confident enough in your friendship to give you his honest opinion. A good friend will tell you when you're out of line, point out when you're being selfish, and confront you when you've been hurtful. Most importantly, though, a good friend will do all of these things in a loving and compassionate way, as prescribed by the apostle Paul in Ephesians 4:15.

A good friend is not easily discouraged in the friendship.

A good friend actually believes that "friends are friends forever." A good friend's loyalty is unwavering. A good friend recognizes and accepts your flaws and weaknesses. A good friend may be hurt by you, but will come to you with that hurt. A good friend will accept your heartfelt apology without holding a grudge. A good friend will not allow your friendship to be jeopardized by trivial (or even not-so-trivial) matters.

A good friend is someone who has taken the time to get to know you.
A good friend is someone who calls you every time *The Breakfast Club* is on
TV because she knows it's your favorite movie. A good friend is someone
who embarrasses you (in a good way) by making a big deal of your birthday,
even when you tried to pretend you didn't want him to. A good friend is
someone who makes you a tape of your favorite songs just because she felt
like doing it. A good friend is someone who listens for the Giants' score every
night, even though he hates sports, because he knows you're a big fan. A
good friend is someone who is interested in things for no other reason than
the fact that you're interested in them. A good friend celebrates you and the
things you love.

THE PERFECT CANDIDATE

HOW TO BE SOMEONE OTHERS WOULD LIKE TO DATE

Entering the dating world is a bit like going back to your old grade school playground. Suddenly the fear of being the last person selected when choosing up sides becomes very real to you again. It's a fear most everyone has experienced at one time or another: "What if no one picks me in the dating game?"

Alas, we don't make the rules of the game, so there's nothing we can do about the "choosy" nature of dating. What we can do is offer you some suggestions as to how you might enhance your dating profile and position yourself as a more obvious choice.

CHECK YOUR AVAILABILITY

Do you know what kind of an attitude you project to other people? You can get a pretty good sense just by watching those around you. Do they seem reluctant to approach you? Do they seem uncomfortable around you? If so, you may be unknowingly thwarting opportunities to meet new people—including those of the opposite sex.

If you're unsure about the signals you're sending to other people, ask your friends for some feedback. Find out what their initial impressions of you were. Did you seem snobby to them? Was there something about you that said, "Don't bother approaching me—I'm not interested"? What did they think? Encourage your friends to be honest and not to worry about sparing your feelings.

You've probably met people who were nothing like they first seemed to you. Could it be that you're that type of person? If so, you're probably going to want to correct people's misconceptions. If you've got an unapproachable exterior, the best way to let people know what you're really like is to approach them. Show them the warm, caring, funny, approachable person beneath the facade.

CHECK YOUR MAGNETISM

"Magnetism" here refers to the characteristics and qualities that other people find attractive. What attributes of yours do people comment on most often? Do you have an engaging personality, an infectious laugh, an ability to make

WOW!

I Wish She Was Available

There was a girl named Beth at church I desperately wanted to date. She was funny, caring—*and beautiful*. No matter how hard I tried to catch her alone, she was always with Alan.

She *came* with Alan. She *left* with Alan. She *talked* constantly with Alan.

They liked each other a lot—you could just tell.

I was ready to cut my losses one day when I asked a friend, "So, when do you think Beth and Alan will get engaged?"

He stared blankly at me, "Engaged!? You're sick."

"Sick? What do you mean? They're practically inseparable," I replied.

"Yeah, of course they are—they're *brother and sister!*"

—Brad, Fair Lawn, NJ

others feel comfortable? How freely do you allow yourself to express those things? Is there something in your life that is prohibiting you from setting your natural attributes loose on the world? If so, address the stumbling block. Ask the Lord to help you recognize your "attractive" features and feel comfortable enough with them to share them with others.

We're not talking about trying to be something you're not. If you're not naturally dynamic, don't try to be. Just make sure you let the good things inside you shine out.

CHECK YOUR SENSE OF HUMOR

If you have a good sense of humor, people will take notice. Looks fade and bodies sag, but a sense of humor is attractive throughout life. We're not talking about being a stand-up comic or having a joke or sarcastic comment ready for every occasion. We're not even necessarily talking about *being* funny. We're talking about recognizing and enjoying humor when you see or hear it. We're talking about having a ready smile when you hear a witty comment whispered under someone's breath during class. We're talking about having a broad enough understanding of American culture to recognize parody when you see it. But most of all, we're talking about making people comfortable with your laugh.

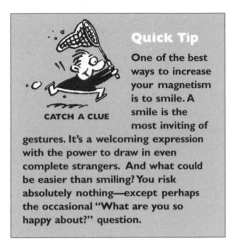

CATCH A CLUE

Quick Tip

One of the best ways to increase your magnetism is to smile. A smile is the most inviting of gestures. It's a welcoming expression with the power to draw in even complete strangers. And what could be easier than smiling? You risk absolutely nothing—except perhaps the occasional "What are you so happy about?" question.

CHECK YOUR APPEARANCE

What we are suggesting here is not that you conform your appearance to meet society's standards of beauty or sex appeal. You don't have to look like a Hollywood star. You don't have to dress in the latest fashions. What you *do* need to do is be the best *you* that you can possibly be.

Take a look at your appearance—your hair, your makeup, your clothes. Think about why you adopted that particular look. Some people choose to wear old, baggy clothes because they're uncomfortable with drawing attention to themselves. Others wear black all the time because they're unsure about mixing and matching colors and styles. Some people have worn their hair a certain way since they were in sixth grade simply because they were afraid to change it. If you've adopted a personal style out of fear, discomfort, or habit, maybe it's time for some changes. Consider experimenting with your look to find out what's really best for you. Talk to hair stylists, makeup experts, and clothing salespeople to help you figure out what would look good on you. If you're comfortable with what you hear, try it. Do what you can to bring out your best features.

ME, MYSELF, AND I

DISCOVERING WHO YOU ARE

Strange though it may sound, self-awareness is perhaps your most valuable attribute when it comes to dating. After all, if you don't know who you are, how can you decide who or what is best for you in a relationship? To help you figure out who you are, we've put together some questions for you to answer.

WHAT'S IN YOUR PAST AND HOW DOES IT AFFECT YOUR PRESENT?

Obviously the place to start here is with your parents. What are (or were) they like? What are your mother's most obvious personality traits? How did those traits affect you as a child? For example, if your mother was a demanding perfectionist, you may have been eager to please her as a child. Do you recognize any of your mother's traits in yourself as an adult? If so, which traits did you inherit? How does it make you feel to know that you inherited those traits?

Along those same lines, ask yourself what strong beliefs your father holds, what absolutes dictate his view of the world. How did those beliefs affect you when you were younger? For example, if he was a strict conservative, did you find yourself gravitating toward liberal causes?

How well do you get along with your parents today? Have you talked to them about the personality traits you share? Have you reconciled any differences you may have had with them in the past? Do you have an adult relationship with them today?

Finally, how do you think your relationship with your parents will affect your dating relationships? If you say, "It won't," you haven't considered the question carefully enough. Do you think you'll choose people whose personality and tendencies mirror those of your mother or father? Or, in the opposite extreme, do you think you'll choose people based on how different they are from your parents?

WHERE ARE YOU GOING?

How do you envision yourself in the future? What do you want to do with your life? What career awaits you? What goals do you want to accomplish? What adventures do you want to undertake? What challenges do you want to face?

These questions are important not only for self-motivation, but also for considering where a dating partner (or future spouse) will fit into your plans.

What Are You Made Of?

CATCH A CLUE

If your body had an ingredient label on it, what would it say? What strengths, gifts, talents, and abilities do you possess? What weaknesses, handicaps, or health problems afflict you? What major fears or insecurities plague you? What tragedies have changed you? What dreams and goals motivate you? What obstacles have slowed your progress? What secrets haunt you? You're going to have to do some serious soul-searching to come up with these answers.

After you've worked up a mini-profile of yourself, create a profile of your "perfect date." Go into as much detail as you can concerning the strengths, abilities, weaknesses, fears, and dreams of your perfect date. Sure, it's only make-believe, but it may be a useful exercise to you. Compare your profile with that of your dream date. How closely do they match? What can you learn about yourself, especially about your dating preferences, from this exercise?

Do you imagine a partner who will share your dreams? Or do you

imagine someone with dreams of his or her own? Are your plans for the future compatible with those of your make-believe partner? Could you live with someone who did not share or even encourage your future interests?

WHAT DO YOU NEED?

What are you missing in your life? What void needs to be filled? (*Note:* If you claim that there is *nothing* missing in your life, then why are you wanting to date?) Which of your needs are not being met as a single person? Do you need a source of stability in your life? Someone to center you? Someone to love you? How do you envision another person (or even a spouse) meeting these needs for you?

Don't underestimate the role that needs play in a dating relationship. Having needs does not make you a needy person. Everyone has needs. The key to dating is finding someone who will fulfill your needs while at the same time you fulfill his or her needs. When two truly compatible people come together, it's like a key and a lock—a perfect fit.

Understanding yourself will go a long way toward understanding the dating choices you make, which, in turn, will help you make better dating choices.

WHAT'S WRONG WITH ME?

WHY YOU MAY NOT BE GETTING ANY DATES

Which is more frustrating: sitting at home waiting for someone to ask you out or constantly being rejected when you ask someone out? We'll call it a tie. Whether you're taking the active route of trying to find someone who'll go out with you or the passive route of waiting for someone to call, remaining dateless weekend after weekend can be a discouraging and sometimes even a humiliating experience.

Why aren't you getting any dates? Let's take a look at some questions that might shed some light on the subject. Answer them as honestly as possible. See if you discover some things about yourself that (a) surprise you, and (b) explain why you may not be getting dates.

Are You Too Scarce?

Where do you spend your free time? If you're at home watching TV every weekend or in the library studying, you really can't expect to be a hot item on the dating circuit. "Out of sight, out of mind" is a credo you should think about. If you're not making yourself visible where people of both sexes hang out and interact, you're limiting your possibilities. You may have to get over your shyness and start spending some time in such "see and be seen" environments as the mall and school functions.

Are You Too Needy?

It's a strange paradox. We all want to be needed, yet most of us tend to shy away from emotionally needy people. Why is that? For many, it's a matter of time and energy. They don't have enough of either to satisfy the emotional void of needy people.

So where do you rate on the neediness scale? Are you the kind of person who prefers to talk to your boyfriend or girlfriend four or five times a night? Do you constantly question people's feelings for you? Are you overly dependent on other people for your emotional well-being? If so, you may need to seek some professional help to get you through your neediness. Most people can spot an emotionally needy person a mile away, giving them plenty of time to steer clear.

Are You Too Choosy?

Is it possible that *you* are the one preventing you from dating? What are you looking for in a date? How important is physical attractiveness? a nice body? wealth? intelligence? a nice car? a good family? the right set of Christian values? How many people have you found who meet your standards? Is it possible that you've raised the dating bar so high that no one can

DON'T FORGET

What to Do While You're Waiting for Mr. or Ms. Right

1. Learn about yourself. Without getting too self-centered, talk to your friends about what they see in you and what they'd like to see *from* you. Find out what you can about what makes you tick (and what makes you "ticked," for that matter).

2. Improve yourself. We are *not* suggesting that you change to please someone else. We're suggesting that you take a good look at yourself—physically, spiritually, emotionally, and intellectually—and identify some areas you would like to work on.

3. Study other people's relationships. Ask your friends and family members what they would do differently if they were single again. Ask them what works in their relationships and what doesn't.

4. Get on with your life. Instead of moping about your singleness, take advantage of it. Recognize that there are things you can do while you're single that you'll never be able to do when there's a significant other in your life. Don't waste your single years just waiting for someone.

make it over? Is it time to reevaluate your dating preferences and standards? Ask the Lord to give you wisdom concerning your dating standards. You certainly don't want to set them too low and start going out with everyone you meet. On the other hand, you don't want to rule out everyone you know.

Are You Too Scary?

Is it possible that you're sitting at home dateless every weekend because people are intimidated by you? What kind of an attitude do you project to your friends and to people you don't know? You can get a pretty good sense of it just by watching those around you. Do they seem reluctant to approach you? Do they seem uncomfortable around you? Don't look now, but you may be unwittingly shooting yourself in the foot when it comes to dating.

Ask your friends about your attitude. Find out what their initial impressions of you were. Did you seem snobby? Were you unapproachable in their eyes? Get the scoop from those you trust. It may be that you're someone who makes a bad first impression. If so, that's okay. You can correct that with a little effort on your part. The key is smiling. A smile is a welcoming gesture that almost immediately puts people at ease. Not only that, it's easy to do (although you may have to retrain the muscles in your face if you're out of practice.)

EXTENUATING CIRCUMSTANCES

SHOULD YOU EVEN BE DATING RIGHT NOW?

Anytime's a good time for a relationship, right? Wrong. There are dozens of circumstances and situations that should make you think twice about hooking up. We've listed some of these circumstances below. If you or the person you're considering dating is going through any of these situations, you might want to call a time-out on the relationship until the matter is resolved.

A Crazy Schedule

Let's face it, there are times in your life when you're just plain overbooked. You've got ten things all clamoring for your time and attention. You can barely think straight. There's nothing you can do about the overload except hang on and wait for it to go away. Sometimes—say, for instance—if you play in a couple of soccer leagues, the crazy schedule may last months. Sometimes it's just a matter of days. Either way, it's no time to be starting a relationship. How flattering is it to say to a would-be date, "I can squeeze you in for half an hour a week from Wednesday"? Just cool the dating until your schedule lightens up.

Pressure at School

If you're in the midst of an academic crunch, the last thing you need is a person in your life to mess up your priorities. It's hard enough to concentrate on school work under the best conditions. Throw in the daydreaming and inevitable phone calls that go along with a new relationship, and you're just asking for trouble. If you're facing midterms or final exams, if you're working on a term paper or special project, or if you're buckling down to avoid a failing grade, put your romantic pursuits on hold until the pressure at school has been dialed back a bit.

Desperation

If you're feeling lost, depressed, sad, or especially lonely, one of the first things you may want to do is reach out for someone else—as in, a romantic relationship. Unfortunately, one of the *last* things you *should* do under those circumstances is start a romantic relationship. How good are you going to be for someone else if you can't help yourself? Don't rush into a relationship, thinking it will help you.

CATCH A CLUE

Avoiding the Rebound

The only time you should be excited about a rebound relationship is on a basketball court. If the person you're considering dating is less than six months out of a serious relationship, you may be asking for trouble. For one thing, you've got the problem of the persistent ex, who's still trying to reconcile things. For another, you've got the "comparison syndrome" to deal with. ("Such-and-such used to call me every night right before I went to bed so that his voice was the last thing I heard before I fell asleep.") Finally, you've got the very real possibility that the person you're dating still has feelings for the ex.

It won't. Your first priority should be to find help for yourself, preferably professional or pastoral help. Then, when you're feeling better, you can start a relationship.

Family Problems

This is a major red-flag area. If your parents or the parents of the person you're considering dating are having marital problems—as in, separation or divorce—put the relationship on the back burner. There are much more important issues for you (or your potential date) to work through. The danger of dating in the midst of family upheaval is that the person going through the crisis is going to be looking for anything that will provide some kind of stability. What happens, then, is that an unnaturally intense connection is formed too early in the dating relationship. Our advice is to postpone the relationship until serious family counseling has been started.

An Important Future Goal

If you or the person you're dating has a major event in the future that you're anticipating and planning for, you may want to hold off on getting serious. We're talking about anything from a short-term overseas opportunity to plans to attend a service academy. You know the old saying: "If you love something, set it free ... yada, yada, yada." There will be plenty of time later in life to pursue your romance, if you choose to. Some opportunities never repeat themselves. Don't give up a potentially life-changing opportunity for a relationship that may last all of two months.

THE IMPOSSIBLE DREAM?

WHEN IS IT OKAY TO COMPROMISE YOUR STANDARDS?

You're probably recoiling in horror at the subtitle of this section. "Compromise my standards? Never! I'd rather stay single forever than compromise my standards!" That's a very noble attitude to take. We wish you all the best in your future singleness.

Standards are an absolute necessity for anyone considering entering the dating world. But if you treat your set of standards like they're the Ten Commandments, engraved in stone with no room for discussion or debate, you may be making a huge mistake. It's a much better idea to cast a critical eye on your standards from time to time, making sure that they continue to reflect who you are and what you want from a dating partner. With that in mind, let's take a look at what it means to compromise your standards.

TO SET THE IMPOSSIBLE STANDARD

At this point in our discussion, we're going to have to bring up a rather unpleasant fact about you. But don't get paranoid. This same fact holds true for (almost) everyone who ever lived. It seems that there is an unfortunate side effect to being human: we're not perfect.

And yet perfection is what some people look for when they set their dating standards. This is what they may have in mind:

Wanted

Single Christian male, 6'2" or taller, 185-187 lbs., with plans to go to medical school, serve a year as a missionary in an African nation, and then become a pediatrician and live in the northwest Chicago suburbs. Must be a nonsmoker, nondrinker, drug-free, and a virgin. Products of broken homes or dysfunctional families need not apply. Interests should include racquetball, golf, sailing, travel, fine dining, holding hands in front of a fireplace, gardening, and Bible reading. Fluency in at least four languages a must; I.Q. above 150 a plus.

Maybe we're exaggerating, but the point is the same. In an effort to protect themselves from bad dating situations, some people set impossible standards for their future partners.

If the people who set those standards aren't much interested in dating, there's no problem. If, however, they're out in the extremely *im*perfect dating world, they may find themselves frustrated by their lack of suitable partners. And it may be time for them to reevaluate their standards.

To reevaluate your dating standards, you need to decide what is nonnegotiable and what is merely a strong preference. After striking out with her rather extreme example above, our intrepid dater may determine that things like height and weight ranges, career plans, geography, and some interests are her *preferences,* not her standards. She may decide not to rule out a possible date candidate just because he's 5'11" or considers Arby's fine dining. As she relaxes her standards a bit, she may discover something rather shocking about herself. She may discover that she *prefers* the company of guys who don't fit her ideal profile, that she enjoys being around people who can introduce her to new things. The young woman's nonnegotiables remained intact, though. She still would not date non-Christians or non-males. She would not date anyone who smoked, drank, or used drugs. She would not date anyone who was not a virgin. Those standards were too important to her to even consider compromising. Other standards, like the one involving people from broken homes or dysfunctional families, she's not sure are non-negotiables—but she's not ready to compromise them yet. She needs to pray and think about it some more.

THE BOTTOM LINE

One More Thing

Don't start reexamining your standards every weekend that you don't have a date. In fact, don't start reexamining your standards until you've spent some time praying and thinking about them. Then, if you're convinced that your standards are nearly impossible to meet, go ahead and compromise—carefully.

COMPROMISE YOUR STANDARDS, NOT YOUR MORALS

We have no idea as to what is important to you in your dating relationships. But we can guess what one of your absolute, non-negotiable standards will be: no sex before marriage. Did we guess correctly? If not, it's time for you to rethink your dating compromises.

God's plan for human beings is to enjoy sex within the marriage relationship. Making love to one's spouse is the perfect fulfillment of God's intent for our sexuality. Sex outside of a marriage relationship is not part of God's plan. Thus, no sex before marriage should be a non-negotiable dating standard. Keep this in mind: compromising your standards should *never* involve compromising your morals or your obedience to God.

SECTION 2
WHAT GOD THINKS

PUTTING GOD FIRST

WHO'S ON FIRST?

As your Sunday school teacher always said: Jesus loves you. That's why He wants first place in your dating life. God never promised to drop into your lap the name and address of the perfect person for you. But He does promise to give you wisdom if you ask: see Proverbs 1:7; James 1:5-8.

GOD'S ON FIRST

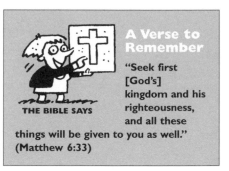

THE BIBLE SAYS

A Verse to Remember

"Seek first [God's] kingdom and his righteousness, and all these things will be given to you as well." (Matthew 6:33)

Who's on first … in your life? Sounds like an Abbott and Costello routine, right? When you think about putting God first, what do you think of? Putting Him first … in everything? in some things? Most of us, if we're honest, think about "assigning" God first place in all of the areas that aren't *quite* so near and dear. In the areas that center around our hearts' desires, we sometimes keep ourselves squarely in the number one position. One such area is the dating life.

Putting God first means loving Him with one's whole heart, mind, soul, and strength, as Jesus commands in Luke 10:27 (see also Matthew 22:37). It means taking the time to ask Him what He wants for your life. It means having no barrier between you and God concerning what you both desire for your life. Why? Because you both desire the same thing—what He wants. Sounds simple? It is—if you call dying to self simple. Because that's what happens when God assumes first place in a life.

Questions to Think About

- How can putting God first change the way you think of dating?
- What are your fears about putting God first?
- What is your "level" of putting Him first in your dating life? (Remember, he already knows. No one else has to know though. This is between you and God.) Check where you fall on the line below.

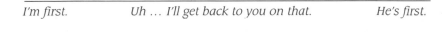

I'm first.   *Uh ... I'll get back to you on that.*   *He's first.*

WIDE ANGLE

Questions for God

What about dating? Putting God first means allowing him to help you make decisions. How can you put God first? For starters, *ask Him.* Keep in mind the five questions a journalist should ask: *who, what, when, where, and how.*

- **Who can I date? Who is right for me?**
- **What is your will for me in dating? (Marriage? To get to know people? To just have fun? To draw closer to you?)**
- **When should I let go of this relationship? When should I ask her to marry me?**

For the superbusy:

- **Where can I find the time to date?**
- **How can I talk about you to the person I date without sounding artificial?**
- **How can I break up with this person without hurting him or her too deeply?**
- **How do I know when I've found the right person?**

Putting God first in dating doesn't mean that God does all the work. He does promise to *be with you* always—but you have to *be someplace* first. That means keeping in touch with Him and trusting that He's working through you.

CHRISTIAN LOVE GUIDES ALL

PRIME MOTIVATION

THE BIBLE SAYS

Keep in Mind

"A new command I give you: Love one another. As I have loved you, so you must love one another." (John 13:34)

Love is an active, in-your-face motivator to do right to someone else.

What is the prime motivator in every Christian's relationship? *Love.* Jesus said, "By [love] all men will know that you are my disciples, if you love one another" (John 13:35). This is not a mushy, gushy, here's-a-box-of-chocolates kind of feeling. Love is an act of your will, a determination to do right by someone, a desire to treat that person as you would yourself.

Okay, you get the picture. We're to love everyone. But what about the "sticky" side of some relationships? How do you show love to a person you *don't* want to date, but who *wants* to date you? How do you show love to someone you *do* want to date, but who has made it definitely clear that he or she does *not* want to date you? How do we show love in a way that *doesn't* encourage the pursuit of a dating relationship, but *does* radiate the love of Christ?

LEARN FROM LOVE

We can all take a lesson from the "Love Chapter"—1 Corinthians 13, verses 4-7: "Love is patient, love is kind. It does not envy, it does not boast, it is not proud. It is not rude, it is not self-seeking, it is not easily angered, it keeps no record of wrongs. Love does not delight in evil but rejoices with the truth. It always protects, always trusts, always hopes, always perseveres."

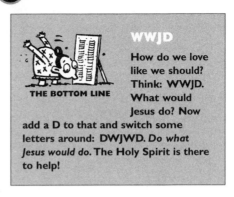

THE BOTTOM LINE

WWJD

How do we love like we should? Think: WWJD. What would Jesus do? Now add a **D** to that and switch some letters around: **DWJWD.** *Do what Jesus would do.* The Holy Spirit is there to help!

- *Love is kind.* Words and actions can be used to build a person up, especially when you have to say "no" to someone (see also Ephesians 4:32; Proverbs 15:1).
- *Love ... is not proud. It is not rude.* Love keeps ego in check.
- *Love ... is not easily angered.* When someone tells you "no," love holds back bitterness.
- *Love ... always hopes, always perseveres.* Love is persistent. It helps us keep on loving, no matter what.

THE "BUT" OF LOVE

But ...

- *Love does not make one a doormat.* Love is firm, not jellyfish soft. Love led Jesus to the cross and it led him to throw the moneychangers out of the temple. You can love, but you don't have to compromise your principles or allow yourself to be manipulated.
- *Love does not give one license to manipulate a person through a kind and "loving" act.* You know the kind: showing "love" to someone to get something in return. We may fool others, but God is never fooled.
- *Love may persevere, but not to the point of annoying someone.* "No" means no. If he or she says no, you'd better back off.

A CHRISTIAN APPROACH TO DATING

STALKING THE WILD DATE

How do you approach dating? Here are a few ways:

And Jesus Said ...

[Jesus] said to them, "Watch out! Be on your guard against all kinds of greed." (Luke 12:15) He was talking about money, but the same advice can be applied to dating.

- *The "predator/prey" approach:* Seeing a potential date as "fair game." A person with this approach likes the challenge of the chase more than the person. He or she makes an art of studying the potential date before moving in for the kill.
- *The "more the merrier" approach:* Going out with as many people as one can to avoid commitment.
- *The "romance roundup" approach:* Pursuing a potential date until he or she is roped and branded in the corral of your love. Yeeehaaaa!
- *The subtle approach:* Making yourself available for someone you want to date, but who is slow about seeking you out. Wherever that person is, you just happen to be near.

A "FRUITFUL" APPROACH

What *is* a Christian approach to dating? Does it just mean dating one person at a time? Ideally, a Christian approach means seeing a person as *a person,* rather than as an object to be won through persistence or through clever study or even as a potential mate right off the bat. It means seeing that person as belonging to *God*. It means taking the time to get to know a person. It means including God in the relationship. How is all of this accomplished? It takes the fruit of the Spirit: "love, joy, peace, patience, kindness, goodness, faithfulness, gentleness, and self-control" (Galatians 5:22-23).

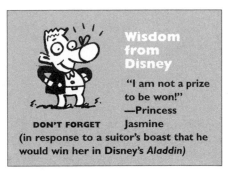

Wisdom from Disney

"I am not a prize to be won!"
—Princess Jasmine

DON'T FORGET (in response to a suitor's boast that he would win her in Disney's *Aladdin*)

- *Love:* Loving God. Loving yourself. Loving others.
- *Joy:* Knowing that the Lord is your strength and that your joy comes from Him.
- *Peace:* The absence of worry. Choosing not to frantically flail about in regard to the relationship. Trusting that God has everything under control. Being at peace does not necessarily mean you won't have struggles as you date. It simply means you are trusting God's leading in your life.
- *Patience:* Taking the time to get to know the person you're thinking about dating or the person you're currently dating. Waiting on God's leading in the relationship, instead of where *you* think the relationship should be.
- *Kindness:* Bending over backward to help a person. Treating your date with respect. There is strength in kindness. Being kind does not make you a doormat. It *does* make you obedient to God.
- *Goodness:* Genuinely wanting what's best for another.
- *Faithfulness:* Being a one-person kind of person. Being loyal.
- *Gentleness:* Giving a soft answer. Avoiding pushiness. There is strength in gentleness, too. Being gentle does not mean you never tell someone no.
- *Self-control:* Not giving in to your own desires. Choosing to follow God's leading. In the dating arena, this is the core of the matter.

BRING HIM ALONG!

1 + 1 + 1 = A GREAT DATE???

The doorbell rings. Ding-dong!

"Who is it?"

"Hi, Pamela. It's me, Jeff."

"Oh, hi. I'm almost ready."

"Good. Say, I'm bringing a friend along. Hope you don't mind."

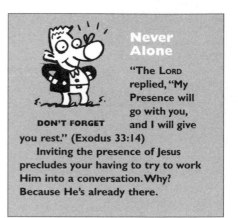

DON'T FORGET

Never Alone

"The LORD replied, "My Presence will go with you, and I will give you rest." (Exodus 33:14)

Inviting the presence of Jesus precludes your having to try to work Him into a conversation. Why? Because He's already there.

Sounds weird? Normally we think two's company and three's a crowd. But when one of the three is Jesus, three can seem kinda cozy.

As Christians, we can't help but take God with us wherever we go. After all, the Holy Spirit has taken up residence in our lives (see 1 Corinthians 6:19-20). But his presence in our lives can sometimes go unacknowledged, particularly in situations when we're trying to make a good impression on the opposite sex.

How can we bring Jesus along on dates?

BRING HIS PRESENCE AND PEACE

If you're out to dinner, praying before the meal is a way to invite His presence. You don't have to wait until food is in front of you to pray, however. You can pray before going out. Ask God to make His presence known. Why is this important? Well, the answer lies with you. If His presence is important to you, His presence is important enough to be made known. With his presence comes peace, the peace "which transcends all understanding" (Philippians 4:7). When you're feeling jittery about a date, peace is a good thing.

BRING HIS WARMTH

Along with God's presence comes the warmth of Jesus. You can share His warmth through a smile or a gentle look. Cultivate a warm, giving attitude. How? Ask the Holy Spirit. Your date will thank you.

BRING HIS SELF-CONTROL

Don't forget that Jesus faced temptation. We may think that because

Ways You Can Bring Him Along

CATCH A CLUE

- If you're out on a walk, comment on the beauty of creation. This is a natural place for a conversation of this kind. Commenting on the beauty of creation at the bowling alley might seem a little forced.
- Ask your date to share his or her thoughts about Jesus.
- Mention God's name in the conversation. As we get to know others, we can't help but mention our close friends in our conversations.

    Therefore ...

    Let your "light" show. Your behavior will naturally invite Christ's presence.

Jesus is God, He doesn't understand the temptations that humans face. Jesus is both God and man. As a man, He was acquainted with temptation (see Matthew 4:1-11). But he promised to help us when we're tempted (see Hebrews 4:14-16). Self-control is one fruit that shouldn't be left on the vine! (see also Galatians 5:22-23).

BRING HIS SENSE OF HUMOR

Bringing Jesus on a date doesn't mean you have to quote Scripture to each other all evening or sit there looking somber. God invented laughter. Jesus was a man of sorrows because of our sin, but He knew joy, too. He probably liked to laugh. He certainly enjoyed being with people. You can, too!

WHAT DOES THE BIBLE SAY ABOUT DATING?

GOD FIRST

You're putting God first. You're letting love guide you. You're bringing Christ on your dates. Now, you ask, what are some biblical principles for dating? Glad you asked. There are no Scriptures that say, "This is the way to date." After all, in the culture of Bible times, marriages were arranged. People did not date. But there are some general principles you can keep in mind. Let's call them the dating "Be-attitudes."

Be Willing to Trust God

"Trust in the Lord with all your heart and lean not on your own understanding; in all your ways acknowledge him, and he will make your paths straight" (Proverbs 3:5-6).

It's easy to lose sight of this truth. We get distracted by our own fears and desires and those of others. Some of the messages we receive breed fear and distrust within us.

- "Get married!"
- "What, you're *still* single?"
- "If you're not in a relationship, something must be wrong with you."

God wants us to place our trust in *Him,* not in our feelings, the messages we hear, or even in our own *faith.*

Be Led by the Spirit

"Be filled with the Spirit" (Ephesians 5:18). Jesus was led by the Spirit in everything he did. Does this mean you can be led by the Spirit and still have fun on a date? You betcha! Being led by the Spirit isn't the end of joy—it's the beginning!

Be Prayerful

"Pray continually" (1 Thessalonians 5:17). In other words, have an attitude of prayer. Prayer can give you the heart guard you need when temptation comes (see also Hebrews 4:16). Prayer also keeps you focused on God and His desires.

Be Wise about Who You Choose to Date

"If any of you lacks wisdom, he should ask God, who gives generously to all without finding fault, and it will be given to him" (James 1:5). God gives us the wisdom to make wise decisions in our relationships. But you don't just gain wisdom when you ask. You gain God's leading as well.

Many Christians use 2 Corinthians 6:14 as the standard for who they should *not* date: "Do not be yoked together with unbelievers." Again, you will need to be wise as well as prayerful.

Be Yourself

"I am fearfully and wonderfully made; your works are wonderful, I know that full well" (Psalm 139:14). You've heard the saying "God made me and doesn't make junk" right? This truth reminds us to be ourselves, to be *real* with those we date. Knowing that we're loved and accepted by God helps.

Be Honest

"Do not lie" (Leviticus 19:11). A lie is one of the quickest ways to kill trust in a relationship. Does that mean you have to tell your date you hate her dress or those striped pants really don't go well with his checked shirt? Not unless your opinion is demanded. If so, use tact or better still, change the subject!

BRINGING YOUR DATE CLOSER TO GOD

CONSULT THE EXPERT

No one knows better than God how to bring a person into a closer walk with Him. Before you meet your date, pray for him or her. Make a habit of praying for that person's spiritual welfare.

Ask God for creative ways to encourage your date into a deeper walk with Christ. Pray *with* your date, too. After all, "where two or three gather together ... I am there among them" (Matthew 18:20 NLT).

ASK ABOUT THEIR WALK WITH GOD

Avoid the "don't ask—don't tell" syndrome. Be prepared to share your own journey. Talk about the ways God has helped you grow. Ask

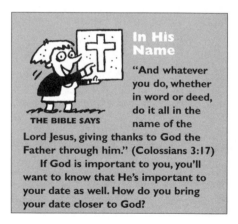

In His Name

THE BIBLE SAYS

"And whatever you do, whether in word or deed, do it all in the name of the Lord Jesus, giving thanks to God the Father through him." (Colossians 3:17)

If God is important to you, you'll want to know that He's important to your date as well. How do you bring your date closer to God?

questions: "What delights you the most about God?" "What are some further areas for growth in your walk?" You can both learn from each other. "As iron sharpens iron, a friend sharpens a friend" (Proverbs 27:17 NLT). Try to keep the conversation upbeat and nonthreatening, rather than reward. After all, you *are* on a date.

Try This

Try this with your date. (Wait until you know the person fairly well.) Both of you can assess where you are by circling a number to show where you are and where you'd like to be in your walk with Jesus. (Each of you will circle two numbers.)

WIDE ANGLE

How important is your walk with Jesus?

1	2	3	4	5	6	7	8	9	10
Not important									*Very important*

How often do you have a "quiet time"?

1	2	3	4	5	6	7	8	9	10
Never have time for one									*Daily*

How would you describe yourself?

1	2	3	4	5	6	7	8	9	10
Stunted in growth									*Growing*

THINK ABOUT STUDYING THE SCRIPTURES TOGETHER

Right there at the dinner table? you might ask. Well … no, unless you really *want* to. Think about a future time when you can get into the Word. You might do this in a group setting with other singles. If you're in the early stages of dating someone, try to avoid jumping into a "couples-oriented" Bible study. Save that for when you're in a deeper relationship. Instead, pick one that keeps the focus on God's character or principles for Christian living.

BE WILLING TO DRAW CLOSE TO GOD YOURSELF

The best way to draw your date closer to God is to draw close to Him yourself. Anything less just seems hypocritical.

TRY TO AVOID TEMPTING SITUATIONS

You know your own temptation threshold. Your date has one too. Talk about your commitment to God and your need to respond to temptation in a godly way. As you both contemplate drawing near to God, expect to be tempted. The key is to keep the lines of communication open. Be honest about the things that tempt you. To minimize temptation, keep in mind this handy phrase: *Don't go there!* Don't hand each other temptation on a tray. For example, if the two of you are alone for a long length of time in a home setting, you're bound to be tempted. Why not meet in a public place or invite others to join you if you have to hang out at home?

SECTION 3
···
ASKING SOMEONE OUT

THE APPROACH

STUDY BREAK

Let's say you've taken a study break while at the campus library. You see someone interesting near the vending machines, someone you don't know very well. You think about going over to talk with the person. How would you approach this person?

So, how *can* you approach someone?

Golden Rule

"Do to others as you would have them do to you." (Luke 6:31)

THE BIBLE SAYS

MAKE EYE CONTACT

Catching a person's eye is the best way to begin. A simple, nonstaring look conveys interest, especially if followed by a smile. Eye contact is only good when you *want* to talk to someone. If you're uncomfortable about someone who is attempting to make eye contact with you, break eye contact and do not follow up with more. If the person persists, make eye contact with a security guard or a burly friend!

ASK QUESTIONS

Questions are good conversation starters. Sometimes they're your best avenue to get to know a person.

BE SINCERE

Sincerity—in this case, a genuine desire to get to know someone—is a great thing. Let the "Golden Rule" (Luke 6:31) be your guide here. If you want someone to be sincerely interested in you, be sincerely interested in that person.

BE FRIENDLY

Friendliness is always attractive. This is a quality that invites conversation. Friendliness says, "I want to get to know you." But use a balanced approach to friendliness. Avoid being overly friendly with people you just met. Here are *some* ways to avoid crossing the line.

THE BOTTOM LINE

Three Strikes and You're Out

Want to come across in a negative way? You will if you come up to bat with these techniques.

Strike 1: *Be arrogant.* Let the person know that you're doing him or her a favor by even talking. Keep the conversation centered on yourself.

Strike 2: *Be impatient.* Keep looking at your watch or looking for someone better looking to come along. Don't waste a lot of time—just get that phone number!

Strike 3: *Be insincere.* Pretend that you're interested in what the person is saying. Communicate only enough interest to get what you want: that person's phone number or to get asked out.

BE HUMOROUS

Humor is a great icebreaker and can defuse a tense situation. Use it often, but use it wisely!

MEETING PEOPLE

JUST A FEW

The army may be "looking for a few good men and women," but so are singles. Where can you meet people? How can you meet people without feeling pressured to ask someone out or to be asked out? Here are a few places and ideas.

At Church

Getting involved at church or within the singles' ministry at church is a good way to simply meet people and explore one's singleness. Many people make lasting friendships through their church involvement. One way to avoid "date" pressure is

WOW!

Looking for a Boyfriend?

An older man stopped to talk to me near the frozen food section of the grocery store. He looked about twenty years older than me. He had a little boy with him, who was probably 10. "Hi," the man said. I returned the greeting, not wanting to be unfriendly. "You lookin' for a boyfriend?" the guy suddenly asked. I stared at him, wondering whether I had heard correctly. He then proceeded to introduce his son to me! I thought, *This guy is looking for a mother for his kid!* I finally said, "No, I'm looking for the frozen food."
—Linda, Carol Stream, IL

to do activities as a group, rather than pairing off. For example, six people might go out for coffee or a pizza. This keeps the focus on the group, rather than on a person.

Some people join singles groups with the obvious intention of finding a mate. While that goal in and of itself is not bad, others might feel pressured. Ask God for wisdom in dealing with the feelings of others and your own intentions.

At the Grocery Store

This is another haunt for some. If you live in a small town, you wind up seeing a number of familiar faces. While you're selecting the perfect orange, it's natural to strike up a conversation with someone. Those conversations are usually short. However, if you just *happen* to keep bumping into the same person in different aisles, well …

At School

This is a natural environment for meeting people. Seeing the same people in classes or at the library promotes relationships. Study groups especially encourage them. But if you don't want to be pressured or pressure someone else, try to avoid singling one specific person out all the time for conversations. If you do fall into a conversation, keep it general (you know the drill) or God-focused.

Is this the one?

Have you ever looked at someone you just met and thought, *Is this "the one"?*

CATCH A CLUE

This is a habit that many singles fall into which makes meeting new people a tense situation. Pray about this tendency if you have it. Trust that when you get to know "the one" you'll realize it without having to ask!

At Work

If you work in an office, you can't help but meet people. Many people pair up with those they meet at work. But if you don't want to be viewed as a potential date right away, keep your conversations work related. Go out to lunch in groups, rather than one-on-one. Keep in mind that work relationships can be sticky at times. Discretion is your best tool.

Professional organizations also allow you an avenue for meeting people. Writers' groups, lawyers' associations, and other career-oriented groups hold conventions where you can get to know others.

THE COURAGE TO CONNECT

ACROSS A CROWDED ROOM

There she is. Or he. Across the room. You're thinking about asking that person out, maybe to join you for coffee. But wait. What's that sound, that thumpa-thumpa-thumpa sound? It's your heart beating fast enough to airlift a freight train. Your knees are knocking so loudly, you're sure they can be heard.

Is that your experience? There's always a risk in getting to know a person—the risk of knowing and allowing yourself to be known. But meaningful relationships are worth the risk. How do you build up courage? Think of the letter *C*—for courage naturally.

Connect with God

Need courage? Ask God for it. He loves you. He even *likes* you. No father likes His children to be fearful and God is no exception. Although asking God for courage is no guarantee that the person will say yes, God does tell us to take our anxieties to Him. "Do not be anxious about anything, but in everything, by prayer and petition, with thanksgiving, present your requests to God" (Philippians 4:6).

Contact a friend

Take an affirmation break. Talking to a good friend is a good way to build up courage. A friend can remind you that you are a wonderful creation of God. Affirmation is not ego stroking, however. Ego stroking keeps the focus on the things that feed your ego: what you look like, how brilliant you are, and so on. Affirmation keeps the focus on what's possible, what God has done, how God has gifted you, and what you can accomplish with God's help. An ego stroke can give you a temporary "high" that can end if you're having a bad hair day. A little bit of affirmation, however, can go a long way.

Affirmation	**Ego Stroke**
You can do this. Trust God.	You da man!
People enjoy talking to you.	You are a chick magnet. Rarrrr!
This is a good way to get to know him.	With your looks, he can't help but say yes.

Cue Your Common Friends

If you and the person you wish to date have friends in common, you can talk to them to find out more about the person. What does he or she like to do? But don't depend on your friends to be your complete source of information or to share details that should only come from your potential date. You might hint to them that that you're interested,

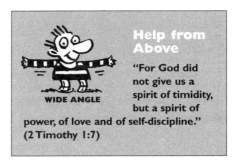

WIDE ANGLE

Help from Above

"For God did not give us a spirit of timidity, but a spirit of power, of love and of self-discipline." (2 Timothy 1:7)

but avoid getting them involved in the actual asking, however. (For more on asking, see "*A* Is for *Ask.*")

Connect with Your Potential Date

Make it a point to be around the person whenever you can. That way, you can engage him or her in casual conversation. The more opportunities you have to talk to the person, the better you'll feel. While you don't want to convey the impression of stalking him or her, you can't make your interest known if you're not around.

A IS FOR ASK

SLEEPLESS … IN YOUR CITY?

Remember in the movie *Sleepless in Seattle* (the perfect *date* movie) how Tom Hanks's character (Sam) worried about asking a woman out? The whole perception of the date changed based on whether he asked a woman out for coffee versus asking her out for dinner. Since he had been out of the dating loop for a while, he wondered how his asking would be perceived.

Can you identify with Sam? If you're wondering how you can keep the pressure and possible embarrassment at bay when asking someone out, read on.

ASKING 101

Find a Common Interest

Do you both like art? sports? music? That can be your "in." "The Monet exhibit is still at the Art Institute. Why don't we go together?" "I've got tickets to the Lakers game on Saturday. Would you like to go?" "There's a concert at the church next Saturday. How about joining me?" The key is to find something you *both like* or something you are *willing* to try. Don't pretend to like something you really dislike. If the person likes opera music and just the *thought* of the Three Tenors makes you gag, try to find another avenue of interest.

Be Confident and Direct

The fear of rejection may loom, but that need not keep you from asking. A question such as "You wouldn't wanna go out with me, wouldja?" does not exude confidence. Even if you don't feel confident, you can still have the confidence that God's presence provides. (See Hebrews 13:5b-6.) Be confident, but not overly so. Saying, "You. Seven o'clock. Dinner. Tonight. Be there," may inspire sarcasm or hostility. A direct approach like "Would you like to have dinner with me this Thursday?" is effective and usually appreciated.

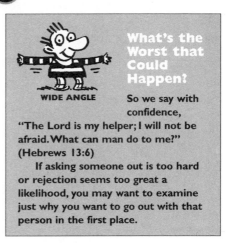

WIDE ANGLE

What's the Worst that Could Happen?

So we say with confidence, "The Lord is my helper; I will not be afraid. What can man do to me?" (Hebrews 13:6)

If asking someone out is too hard or rejection seems too great a likelihood, you may want to examine just why you want to go out with that person in the first place.

Be Definite, Rather Than Vague

When you ask someone out, try to have something definite in mind. "How about sharing a pizza with me?" is definite. "Wanna go out someday?" is vague. This statement may cue you to the person's interest, but it will mean asking the person out a *second* time to make definite plans. So, save yourself the hassle by making your intentions plain the first time. You might choose a day, a place, or a time. Allow for input from the person you ask.

Avoid Game Playing

Statements like, "Suppose I were to ask you to go out with me. What would you say?" may give you an out if you're not sure your interest is reciprocated by someone. But *suppose* is a verbal form of hide-and-seek. It tells the person that he or she isn't worth the possible risk to your ego. Avoiding game playing means you respect yourself and the person you want to date enough to be honest and direct.

Choose a "Safe" Place

Sometimes the asking is hampered by the pressure of having to set up the "perfect date." If so, put aside thoughts of a fancy French restaurant. Instead, choose a "safe," no-pressure environment for your first "outing." A drink at a coffee shop. A walk along the lake. These are inexpensive, let's-talk-and-get-to-

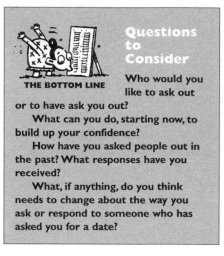

THE BOTTOM LINE

Questions to Consider

Who would you like to ask out or to have ask you out?

What can you do, starting now, to build up your confidence?

How have you asked people out in the past? What responses have you received?

What, if anything, do you think needs to change about the way you ask or respond to someone who has asked you for a date?

know-one-another events. You might agree to meet at the chosen locale as another way to keep the pressure off. (For more creative ways to ask, see "Asking with Style.")

AVOID

Getting an Eligible Friend (same sex as you) or Any Third Party to Do the Asking for You

Cyrano de Bergerac had troubles in this department and you may too. If your friend has more contact with your potential date, the two may hit it off!

Including God as Part of the Deal

One individual was overheard to say, "God told me that we were to get together," when he asked a woman out. A statement such as this is unfair and unworthy of God—don't put words in God's mouth!

ASKING WITH STYLE

CREATIVE ASKING

Our Creator has given us the capacity to be creative. What's the most creative way you've ever heard used to ask someone out? Can't think of one? Well, here are a few. Note: Make sure your potential date has a sense of humor before attempting any!

- Hire a plane, the kind that trails banners across the sky.
- Write the phrase "It is not good for the man to be alone" (Genesis 2:18) on an invitation card, along with your request for a dinner date.
- If you have access to your potential date's computer, record your message as a "sound bite" and load it onto the computer. Assign the "sound" to one of the computer's functions: menu maximizing/minimizing; emptying the "recycler" and so on. Or, create a screen saver with your message.
- Lease a billboard in your area. Some companies will even paint messages on benches.

- If your potential date and you attend the same church, have one of the ushers slip him or her a message folded into the bulletin.
- Send an e-mail card. Some card companies have web sites (for instance, www.bluemountain.com) where you can create a card to send for free or small cost.
- Write your message on a piece of paper, then cut it into puzzle pieces. Slip these into an envelope and send it to your potential date. (A card company like Current, Inc. sells blank forms you can write on. They are already perforated in puzzle-shaped pieces.)
- Place an ad in the daily paper that

your potential date reads.

- If you and your potential date are in the same class, ask the teacher to end class with your request. Make sure (A) your potential date is a good sport; (B) you pretty much know the answer will be "yes"; and (C) you don't mind the presence of witnesses.

- Make signs on the computer and post them around your potential date's dorm, sorority/fraternity house, or in the hallway of the building where he/she has his/her first class.

- If you are in a campus choir, enlist some of the members to "sing" your message outside your potential date's window.

- Send a "thinking of you" card via snail mail, then follow up with a phone call.

- If you work in the same office, place on your potential date's desk a rose with a note attached.

- Politicians put up signs along the road when they're running for office. You might put up signs along the route that your potential date drives to work or stake a sign on his or her front lawn.

- Send your potential date an inter-office memo requesting a date. Make the memo look as official as possible. (There's a risk that your potential date might let the memo sit in his/her in box for a while.)

- Obtain a menu from a restaurant and send it to your potential date with a note: "What would you order for dinner, say this Saturday night at 7?"

- Send a message via a delivery company that sends costumed staffers. Won't your potential date be surprised when a gorilla shows up with your message? A word to the wise: Check with your potential date's boss before having a message delivered to his or her job. Some places of employment frown on frivolity. Getting your potential date fired is a creative way to *prevent* having him or her go out with you.

- Call the radio station your potential date listens to and ask the disc jockey to deliver your message.

GO FOR IT!

BARRIERS

Every hurdler worth his or her salt has to know how to clear a hurdle. Otherwise, he or she will never make it to the finish line. Our own fears or other circumstances are the hurdles that we need to cross in order to connect with others.

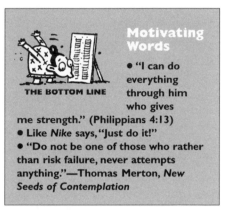

THE BOTTOM LINE

Motivating Words

● "I can do everything through him who gives me strength." (Philippians 4:13)
● Like *Nike* says, "Just do it!"
● "Do not be one of those who rather than risk failure, never attempts anything."—Thomas Merton, *New Seeds of Contemplation*

Fear

In the dating arena, fear of rejection is a major hurdle. To overcome it, you first need to face it. Then seek God's help to deal with it. "Cast all your anxiety on him because he cares for you" (1 Peter 5:7). (See also "The Courage to Connect.")

Lack of Knowledge about a Person

Let's face it—getting to know a person takes work. Patience, love, and persistence can help in your quest to know others. (See Colossians 1:11.) If you're just getting to know a potential date, you might start off by calling or e-mailing the person. Later, you might suggest a no-pressure, this-is-not-a-date coffee session as a date "road test."

Biases or Hidden Agendas

Sometimes there are hurdles we expect the other person to jump. These are our own biases or hidden agendas. "I don't really like her hair. If she'd cut it, I'd ask her out." "He needs to get in the Word more. Then I could really like him." A dose of the Savior's love can clear this hurdle. While some issues are important, others are less earth-shattering. God does not want us to nitpick (see Matthew 7:1-5), but he does expect us to be wise (see Proverbs 8).

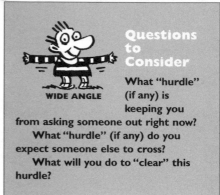

WIDE ANGLE

Questions to Consider

What "hurdle" (if any) is keeping you from asking someone out right now?

What "hurdle" (if any) do you expect someone else to cross?

What will you do to "clear" this hurdle?

Nervousness

If just the thought of asking someone out causes your palms to feel sweaty and your throat to go dry, you're in good company. To combat nervousness, pray first. Then practice what you're going to say before you talk to your potential date. When you're face-to-face (or telephone-to-telephone) with the person, take a deep breath. That can help you control your breathing and feel calmer.

SECTION 4
....
ONCE YOU'VE BEEN ASKED

"NO" PROBLEM

THE "NO" CLINIC

Welcome to the "No" Clinic: the place where you can learn to say no gracefully. At the "No" Clinic, you learn to

- Think of the other person,

- Say "No" in a nice way, and

- Be firm in your decision.

Press any key to continue... .

As we said before, being told "no" never feels great. Yet, there may be times when you'll have to say no to a would-be date. So ... how *do* you say no to someone and still seem like a nice person?

PUT YOURSELF IN THAT PERSON'S PLACE

Take a deep breath. Exhale. Now say Luke 6:31 to yourself: "Do to others as you would have them do to you." In other words, identify with that person. This is *not* to prevent you from saying no. It's just a reminder to treat the other person the way you would want to be treated—gently and respectfully.

In other words, "let him or her down easily" if you can. For example: "Thanks for asking, but I'm going to have to decline." If more of an explanation is required: "You're a nice person, but I don't think we're right for each other. Thanks anyway." The point is to let the person know in a gentle, but *definite* way that you're not interested. This brings up the next point.

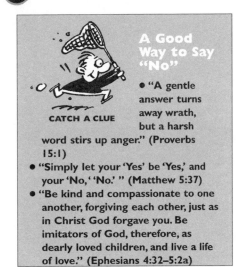

A Good Way to Say "No"

CATCH A CLUE

- "A gentle answer turns away wrath, but a harsh word stirs up anger." (Proverbs 15:1)
- "Simply let your 'Yes' be 'Yes,' and your 'No,' 'No.' " (Matthew 5:37)
- "Be kind and compassionate to one another, forgiving each other, just as in Christ God forgave you. Be imitators of God, therefore, as dearly loved children, and live a life of love." (Ephesians 4:32–5:2a)

BE FIRM

If you're *sure* you don't want to go out with this person, make sure there is no ambiguity in your answer. Telling the person "some other time" creates the impression that the person *could* ask you out again. If, however, you *do* want the person to ask you out, "some other time" works.

A firm no means you're not allowing the other person to talk you into doing something you don't want to do. Sometimes people wind up going out with someone they might have said no to because they're afraid of hurting the other person's feelings. Yet the hurt is far worse when a person knows you're dating him or her because you don't know how to say no.

REVIEW WHY YOU WANT TO SAY NO

Reminding yourself why you're saying no can help you be firm. A review can also help you come up with a tactful explanation if the person asks for one.

Although you don't have to *justify* why you don't want to go out with a person, you might have to nip further invitations in the bud. You can do this by prayerfully considering your reasons. Why prayerfully? To avoid hurting the other person unduly; to ask God to help you know what to say; to make sure you're being honest with yourself.

AVOID TURNING SOMEONE DOWN IN FRONT OF A THIRD PARTY

You don't want to embarrass the person, even if he or she demands an answer in front of a third party. Instead, ask him or her to step to a more private location, or tell the person you'll talk to him or her later. Then do so.

DON'T BEAT YOURSELF UP

Guilt is probably the number one cause of keeping people from saying no. Sometimes the guilt is inflicted upon us by the people we turn down. Sometimes the guilt comes from our own fear that we're somehow being unfair to the other person. Either way, this guilt isn't good. Effective guilt helps us repent when we've sinned. It's an acknowledgment that we're in the wrong. Saying no to a person does not fall into the guilt category.

READY ... OR NOT?

YOUR OUTER APPEARANCE

Your date's tonight. You need to get ready. Not only is your outside appearance important, your inside appearance is too. Let's start with the outside. What will you wear? You want to look your best. But of course, you don't want to look too eager. How can you decide what to wear?

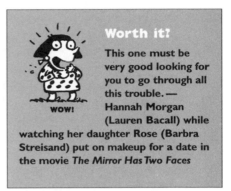

Worth it?

This one must be very good looking for you to go through all this trouble. — Hannah Morgan (Lauren Bacall) while watching her daughter Rose (Barbra Streisand) put on makeup for a date in the movie *The Mirror Has Two Faces*

WOW!

Go for comfort ... and taste. Your destination will decide your attire. If you're going out to the movies, you might dress more casually than you would if you were headed to a nice restaurant for dinner. The key is to look your best ... and look relaxed. So that old bridesmaid dress, the Valentino original, or the Armani suit might be too much, even if you look stunning in it. If you're seeing the person for the first time, you'll already be nervous enough, so wear something you feel comfortable in. (No, not that old bathrobe and those old biker shorts. Something a *little* more upscale.) Wear your favorite color. Wear that shirt that brings out the color of your eyes. You can look great without looking like you spent hours doing it (even if you did).

Impress, but don't excess. If your accessories or outfit is too fussy, you may be trying too hard. Remember, your date is already impressed with you, otherwise he or she wouldn't have asked you out. With that in mind, avoid over accessorizing. You know: the 55 constantly clinking bracelets that match your outfit, that Rolex watch you can see a mile away, that intricate hairdo that needs a team of hairstylists to maintain.

If you happened to catch the movie *The Mirror Has Two Faces,* you'll recall the scene where Barbra Streisand's character, Rose, met Greg (Jeff Bridges) for their first date. Having carefully arranged her hair (including extra hair-pieces), Rose wound up at the restaurant after a wild cab ride with hair sliding off of her head and looking, as she explained, as if she'd been "attacked by wolves." Hey, it *could* happen! (Well ... not the wolves part, but you get the idea.)

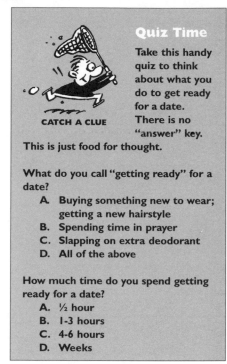

CATCH A CLUE

Quiz Time

Take this handy quiz to think about what you do to get ready for a date. There is no "answer" key. This is just food for thought.

What do you call "getting ready" for a date?
  A. Buying something new to wear; getting a new hairstyle
  B. Spending time in prayer
  C. Slapping on extra deodorant
  D. All of the above

How much time do you spend getting ready for a date?
  A. ½ hour
  B. 1-3 hours
  C. 4-6 hours
  D. Weeks

YOUR INNER APPEARANCE

The way you look on the inside is just as important as the way you look on the outside. (Yes, really!) Before you go out, put off attitudes that are less than God's best and put on those that will promote a great evening. For example:

Put On	**Put Off**
Gratitude	Hey, I'm doing him/her a favor by going out
A servant's heart	Getting all that I can
Grace	The expectation of perfection
Trust in God	Anxiety

Scriptures you can use to get your "inside" ready:

Romans 12:9-13   Philippians 4:5-9

Galatians 5:22-23   Colossians 3:12; 4:6

HOW DO YOU SPELL R-E-L-A-X?

How much you like a person + how nervous you are = pre-date pressure. So before you leave for your date, try to do something you probably don't think is possible: *relax.* Relaxation can take some of the pressure off. How do you relax before a date? Here are some suggestions:

- Watch a movie you like
- Read the Bible (see the Scriptures above for getting your inside ready)
- Play a game on the computer
- Read a book
- Take several deep breaths (but be sure you exhale!)
- Pray
- Take a nap (but don't do a Rip Van Winkle!)
- Have a cup of herbal tea
- Play a sport that relaxes you
- Listen to a CD you like
- Talk to a good friend
- Take a nice, long bath or shower

GREAT EXPECTATIONS

WHAT'S UNDER THE TREE?

What does a person whose thoughts are on Christmas, a person about to go on a date, and a person waiting for the Super Bowl all have in common? Expectations. You know, those little preconceived ideas we have about an anticipated event— the ones we sometimes pretend we *don't* have. They come in three sizes:

That's a Bad Date

I hadn't dated anyone in awhile. Finally HE asked me out—the best looking guy at the office. I was so nervous, I kept expecting the worst to happen. I mean, I could hardly believe he would ask *me* out! Well, the worst did happen. First, I acted like a klutz at the restaurant and spilled coffee all over myself. Then, his old girlfriend saw us together and demanded to get back with him. He left me right there in the restaurant and went off with her!—Sara, Kearny, NE

WOW!

great (high), *average* (not too high/too low), and *terrible* (low). They can seem realistic or implausible: *I expect my date to meet all of my emotional needs.* Or *I really like this person! This whole evening should be perfect!* Or *I'm going out with him for the first time. I don't know what to expect.*

The power of an expectation can cause you to soar or crash and burn into disillusionment if it doesn't pan out. When you're thinking about dating someone in particular or just thinking about the *idea* of dating, take time to consider your expectations. What are your expectations … about the person you plan to date? about the evening itself? about dating in general? Are they high? low? realistic? unrealistic? Do you honestly think the person you date can meet them?

Use the quiz on the next page to see what expectations you might have about dating in general. Circle the response that comes closest to how you feel.

1. You've just arranged a date with someone you really like. You:

A. expect the evening to be perfect.

B. expect the worst to happen—it usually does on dates.

C. expect to enjoy the evening.

2. You've made plans to go out with someone who has been "just a friend" so far. When you think about the date, you:

A. expect the friendship to end if the evening doesn't go well.

B. don't expect any awkwardness; after all, you *are* friends.

C. expect to feel a little nervous, now that you're going out.

3. You're about to date someone after being out of the dating loop awhile.

A. You expect you'll need time to get used to dating.

B. You don't expect this date to be any better than past dates you've have.

C. You expect to jump back into dating easily—after all, it's like riding a bike.

4. If you don't already have a date: When you think about dating, you expect to date:

A. someone who looks like Brad Pitt/Tyra Banks (no exceptions).

B. someone who's fun to be with.

C. someone with a pulse—he/she doesn't have to look good.

5. When you're on a date, you expect to be treated with respect:

A. all of the time.

B. some of the time.

C. at no time.

Use the points to score your quiz.

1. A: 5   B: 1   C: 3
2. A: 1   B: 5   C: 3
3. A: 3   B: 1   C: 5
4. A: 5   B: 3   C: 1
5. A: 5   B: 3   C: 1

18–25: You have high expectations that may not be met. Take time to pray before you leap.

10–17: You have realistic expectations about dating. (But still take time to pray!)

5–9: You have low expectations about dating. Consider whether you really *need* to date someone right now. If you've just gone through a break up or are on the rebound, you might need time to heal before getting back on that horse.

Now consider this

"Trust in the Lord with all your heart and lean not on your own understanding" (Proverbs 3:5). God wants us to trust *Him*, not our fears or feelings. He also wants our hopes to rest in His plans, rather than ours.

Knowing your expectations can expose your fears and provide a useful reality check. Trusting God can keep you from soaring too high or heading for a fall.

MR. OR MS. WRONG

Suppose someone asked you out and you said yes. Just before you go out, however, you make a major discovery: you think this person is "wrong" for you. What do you do?

Interpret the Degree of "Wrongness"

A minor wrong? How "wrong" is this person for you? Does the person have a quality that you cannot stand? Does he or she make you feel uncomfortable? Is he or she "wrong" (to your mind) in his or her way of thinking? Since each person evaluates this for himself or herself, the definition of *wrongness* can seem subjective. If the "wrongness" is relatively minor ("His laugh drives me crazy"; "I don't like what she said about Henri Nouwen"), you need to decide how much the quality unnerves you or whether it could be endured for one evening.

If you currently have a specific issue in mind, choose one of the numbers below to rank how you feel about it.

1	2	3	4	5	6	7	8	9	10
Minor annoyance					I couldn't endure one minute of this				

If the concern is relatively minor and you already agreed to go on the date, then go. Don't renege on your word. But don't accept another invitation to go out.

A major problem. If the concern involves a major issue, that's a different matter. What's of major concern to you? You decide.

I'm a Christian and I just found out my date is not.

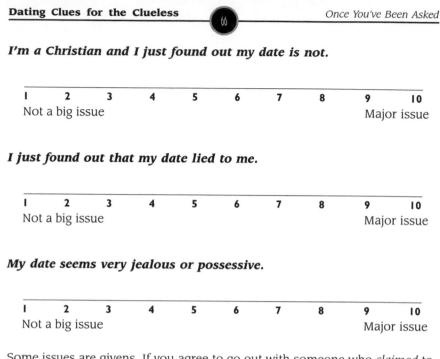

| I | 2 | 3 | 4 | 5 | 6 | 7 | 8 | 9 | 10 |
Not a big issue   Major issue

I just found out that my date lied to me.

| I | 2 | 3 | 4 | 5 | 6 | 7 | 8 | 9 | 10 |
Not a big issue   Major issue

My date seems very jealous or possessive.

| I | 2 | 3 | 4 | 5 | 6 | 7 | 8 | 9 | 10 |
Not a big issue   Major issue

Some issues are givens. If you agree to go out with someone who *claimed* to be single but who turns out to be married or separated, you already know that dating him or her is out. (See Exodus 20:14; Matthew 19:18.) A person who is *separated* is still off limits.

Whatever the issue is, if it strikes a major chord within you . . .

PRAY ABOUT IT

Ask the Lord to give you wisdom. He is always glad to help you make a wise decision. (See Proverbs 1:2-7; 2:–22; 4:5-9; 9:1-12; James 1:5.)

GET OUT OF IT GRACEFULLY

If you unknowingly agreed to date someone with whom you're now having second thoughts (and you know conclusively that you should not go out with him or her), try to back out gracefully. Apologize for any hurt feelings and give an explanation. Don't leave him or her in the dark.

Why apologize? To acknowledge hurt feelings for one thing. For another, to acknowledge that some issues *should have been* discussed beforehand—*before* a date was accepted. If you accepted a date with a person, then asked *afterward* whether he or she was a Christian, your backing out of the date may cause hard feelings. A sincere apology will help. For example, "I know I said I'd go out with you. I'm sorry, but I would prefer not to date someone who isn't a Christian. I don't mean to hurt your feelings." You *do not* have to apologize for having principles. You *are* obligated to "let your light shine before men, that they may see your good deeds and praise your Father in heaven" (Matthew 5:16). That includes treating others the way you would want to be treated (Luke 6:31). If the person lied to you, however, he or she owes *you* an apology. A relationship built on lies won't last.

KNOW WHEN TO GO FOR HELP

Some issues of "wrongness" have to do with a person who may be trouble. (For help in discovering the signs of a person who might be trouble, look at "Warning!") In cases such as this, be prepared to seek help if the person won't take no for an answer. Tell a friend first. If further assistance is needed, don't be afraid to seek help.

JUST SAY NO!

WHEN THE RED FLAGS ARE FLUTTERING

The person of your dreams just asked you out. You want to say yes, but everything within you is crying, "Don't do it!" When should you say no even when you want to say yes?

- When the person isn't a Christian and you know that Christianity is *not* something you're willing to settle about.
- When you or the person you're dating is in it for the wrong reason (to make someone jealous; because you're on the rebound.
- When you know someone is wrong for you.
- When you know that person brings out the worst in you.
- When you feel "uncomfortable" about a person.
- When godly friends or family members tell you to say no. Sometimes a friend can see something you can't see.
- When your potential date's personality clashes in a major way with yours.
- When you want to change the other person. "He has so much potential. If I go out with him, I'd whip him into shape." "She's so much like my ex-girlfriend. I can get her to change." If the words *I can change* _____ (fill in the blank) come to mind, think of another word: *No.*
- When you know the person is still seeing someone else. If you don't like being part of a "corral" of dates, don't join the herd.
- When the person has a past you cannot ignore. Jesus does promise forgiveness for our sins. But sometimes our sins involve consequences that we live with for decades.

SEARCHING TO FIND "THE ONE"

MY ONE AND ONLY?

The "one." Should you only date those who could be "the one"? Should you pass up a date with someone you might like, but whom you don't think you'll marry?

Some Christians date with a goal: to get to know someone who could be a potential spouse. Others just date to get to know people and have fun. What is your goal? In the book *I Kissed Dating Goodbye*, author Joshua Harris stresses the value of "seeking smart love." What's smart love? Not dating a person you know you'd never marry. Not dating until you know you're serious about commitment and seeking a spouse.

"So, how would I know the person *isn't* the one unless I date him or her?" you may ask. "Sometimes you don't know someone isn't the one until you go out with him or her. So that

Would've, Should've ...

WOW!

I knew I should've told Eric no. I was on the rebound from a relationship. I *did* like Eric ... sort of. So, I went out with him. Then I went out with him again. Every time, I felt more and more uncomfortable. I knew he liked me more than I liked him. I liked him as a friend, not as a boyfriend.

I kept hearing the Holy Spirit speak to me. "Are you *sure* this is what you want?" I kept telling myself, *Yes; this is what I want.* Finally, the message changed from "Are you sure this is what you want?" to the *knowledge* that I was hurting Eric by going out with him. I never thought that I had led him on. But I had.—Linda, Tampa, FL means I might have to go out with a lot of this-*ain't*-the-ones, right?"

Is that your view? The fact is none of us will truly know what to do about dating (or anything else in life) if we don't stay in tune with God and our own expectations or agendas. Everything we do has a purpose. Our main purpose for being here is to glorify God, just as Jesus did (see John 15:8). When we live for Christ, He gives us His wisdom to make decisions. That wisdom is definitely needed in the dating arena. How can we use this wisdom in dating? We can use it by . . .

Praying About Our Dating Choices
A prayer like "Help me choose wisely" can help. If you went to college, more than likely you prayed for wisdom to choose the best school for you. You can do this for dates as well. Many times we're hesitant to pray because we're afraid (a) God will give us someone we know we *don't* like; (b) God will *actually* give us someone we *do* like, but we're not really *ready* to make a commitment to anyone. God never promised to force an unappealing gift on His children. As Jesus said, "If you sinful people know how to give good gifts to your children, how much more will your heavenly Father give good gifts to those who ask him" (Matthew 7:11 NLT). In the same token, God never promised to *force* a gift on His kids. God knows all of us quite well. He knows when we're ready to receive a gift and when we just *think* we're ready.

Not Worrying
Worry automatically jams the frequency between you and God. Jesus said, "Do not worry" several times in Matthew 6:25-34. Many times we worry because we're not *really* sure God will help us make good decisions.

SECTION 5
THE ACTUAL DATE

DATING ETIQUETTE

WHAT'S GOOD ETIQUETTE?

What is etiquette? Some might define etiquette as the polite way of doing things. Certainly Miss Manners and Emily Post would agree. There is a dating "etiquette," some of which is unspoken. Traditionally, the man assumed the burden of a date: the planning and execution of it. He would call for his date and convey her to the agreed-upon place. He would hold open all doors—car or otherwise—for her and generally be attentive.

Although women are now asking men out on dates, there are certain rules of etiquette that are still preferred while some might have changed.

THE PERSON WHO SUGGESTS THE DATE PAYS FOR IT

A general assumption is that the person who suggests the date (the where and the how) is the one to pay for it. So, if a woman asks a man out for a date, she is expected to pay. (This is *not* always the case, however.) Some men don't mind a woman paying, others may balk. You might ask your potential date how he or she feels about the topic before the actual date. Don't wait until the check comes to have a discussion.

CRITICIZING "GOOD HOME TRAINING" IS A FAUX PAS

"Good home training"—the values Mom and Dad instilled within you—should not be criticized. A man can *still* be polite and hold open doors for a woman even in the 90s. A woman can also occasionally hold a door open for a man. Regardless of who gets the door, criticizing the person who opens it is rude. The polite response is always, "Thank you."

Small Talk or ...

"What are your favorite movies? Are you from a big family? Where'd you go to college?"

"What are you doing?"

"I'm making date talk."—Maggie Winters to her date Sonny on *Maggie Winters*, a sitcom on CBS

WOW!

COMPLIMENTS YES; FLATTERY NO.

A compliment is a *sincere* expression of appreciation; flattery is insincere praise. If you notice something nice about your date, be sure to compliment him or her. Avoid compliments that could make the person uncomfortable. Do not comment on something you know you don't like; that is flattery. If you're being complimented, the polite response is "Thank you" rather than "Oh, that's not true" or "This old thing? I've had it for years."

GET TO KNOW EACH OTHER

The whole purpose of a date is to get to know each other. This is usually done by talking and asking each other questions. (Really!) Therefore, if your date asks you questions about yourself, she expects you to talk about yourself and expects you to be interested enough to ask her about herself. Monosyllabic answers will not carry the conversation very far. For example: "So, what do you do?" "Work." "How was your day?" "Okay." The conversation needs both parties' input. If you're dating someone who is painfully shy, you might need to work harder at the conversation. If you're naturally talkative, you may need to monitor whether you're allowing your date to give enough input.

A THANK YOU IS A GOOD THING

If you've enjoyed yourself on the date, you can show your appreciation by expressing your thanks. "I had a great time. Thanks." "I like this restaurant. Thanks for bringing me here." Don't expect your date to read your mind. If you appreciated his or her companionship, say so.

MEN AND WOMEN ARE DIFFERENT

No kidding! With that in mind, try to understand where your date is coming from. If he's a "traditional" sort, he might want to do chivalrous things like open doors, hold out chairs as a sign of his interest.

CATCH A CLUE

Details

"My dear Martha, you are so upset over all these details!" (Luke 10:41 NLT) Jesus gently chided Martha, the original "Happy Homemaker" over her single-minded focus on the work detail and her "role" as hostess. Mary, however, chose the "good" part of the experience: the enjoyment of Jesus' presence. Many of us might be "Marthas" when it comes to dating. We focus more on the "details" of the date and what our "role" is, instead of actually enjoying the experience. Is that your experience?

He may feel strongly about this role, and may register confusion if the woman takes on his perceived role. If she's a "traditional" sort, she may *expect* you to hold open doors and perform other attentive acts as a sign of your affection for her. If she's not "traditional," she may open doors for *you*. The key is to be willing to learn how the other feels. If you're a nontraditional sort, could you live with your date's need for tradition? If not, you need to evaluate why you wish to date this person. When in doubt, ask rather than assume.

A GREAT DATE

WANT TO HAVE A GREAT DATE?

- Feel good about yourself.
- Compliment your date in some way. Let him or her know how much you like and respect him/her.
- Smile from the heart often. "A cheerful look brings joy" (Proverbs 15:30).
- Encourage laughter throughout the evening.
- Be a good conversationalist. Encourage your date to talk about himself or herself. Ask questions.
- Keep an upbeat, cheerful attitude, even if the movie turns out to be lousy or the food isn't all that great. After all, your date's not to blame.
- Be polite. Hold your date's door open (this is not limited to males). Don't balk at chivalry. If a chair is held out for you, by all means sit in it.
- Don't crowd the evening with an itinerary of activities. ("First, we'll go here; then we'll stop off here; then we'll …") Instead, go someplace where you can feel relaxed and get to know one another at leisure.
- In the same token, don't schedule a date before a high-pressure event. For example, arranging to meet someone before you have a final or before you have to go to a meeting of some kind. Your mind will be on the event, rather than on the person.
- Let the "real you" come through.
- Be sure to tell your date thanks for the evening. Make sure he or she knows how much you enjoyed his/her company. Chances are … you will again.

HOW TO HAVE A MISERABLE TIME

HOW TO HAVE A ROTTEN TIME

Want to have a really bad date? Here's how:

- Insult your date in some way. Comment that her haircut looks awful, his suit is tacky, or that his car has seen better days. And don't forget to make a dig about his or her intelligence.

- Talk about past boyfriends/ girlfriends. Go on and on about them: how nice they are, how great looking they are.

- Complain all evening. Whine about the movie, the restaurant, or some other aspect of the date. Make sure your date knows how bad the service was, how pathetic the script of the movie was (and how you could write a better one), and so on.

- Name drop. If you ever met a celebrity, be sure your date knows this.

WOW!

A Dress or a Shower Curtain?

I had an expensive banquet date ruined on account of my best friend. We were double-dating and picking up our dates. We were at my date's house and she entered the room wearing an expensive satin gown. Before I had a chance to tell her how beautiful she looked, my friend blurted out, "Ha! Your dress looks like a shower curtain!"

All of us starred at my friend in disbelief and he immediately knew he should have kept his mouth shut—but it was too late. The damage was done.

The rest of the evening I spent trying to compliment my date, but her confidence was long gone. She wasn't much company that night, and my friend learned that what you say *can* make a difference.

—Donald, Cape Cod, MA

- Act in a arrogant manner. Make sure your date knows whether you're "slumming" to date him or her.
- Insult your date's church or congregational affiliation. Let him or her know how "wrong" that church or denomination is about "the truth."
- Make sure the conversation centers around you, you, you! Make sure you don't offer your date a compliment or ask him or her to talk about himself/herself. While you're at it, make sure your date does not discover the "real" you—just the aspects you *want* him/her to know.
- By all means, *don't* thank your date for taking you out. After all, that person ruined your entire evening. This behavior should not be rewarded.

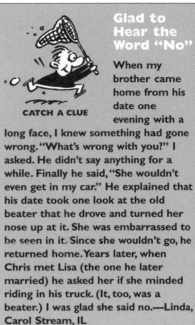

CATCH A CLUE

Glad to Hear the Word "No"

When my brother came home from his date one evening with a long face, I knew something had gone wrong. "What's wrong with you?" I asked. He didn't say anything for a while. Finally he said, "She wouldn't even get in my car." He explained that his date took one look at the old beater that he drove and turned her nose up at it. She was embarrassed to be seen in it. Since she wouldn't go, he returned home. Years later, when Chris met Lisa (the one he later married) he asked her if she minded riding in his truck. (It, too, was a beater.) I was glad she said no.—Linda, Carol Stream, IL

WHAT DID YOU EXPECT?

MEETING EXPECTATIONS

Okay, now that you've dealt with your own date expectations, it's time to deal with those of the person you're dating. (Hey, if you have them, he or she does too.) How do you deal with high expectations? low ones? unspoken ones? What do you do when your date's expectations aren't met? *Should* you be the one to meet them?

Oops!

WOW!

I expected her to be on time, to be enthusiastic, to be herself. At least that's the person I thought I was going out with, 'cause that's how she seemed at work. Boy, was I wrong.—Ernest, Hope, ID

EXPECTATIONS THAT CAN BE MET

There are certain expectations that are "givens" in the dating relationship; for example, treating each other with respect, rather than behaving rudely. Another "given" is expecting the person you date to be himself/herself and vice versa. If these expectations aren't met, you might want to rethink whether you wish to date this person again.

If your potential date has gotten to know you a little before you go out, he or she expects a certain *you* to show up on the night of the date. A sudden drastic change in hairstyle, personality, or other major changes could be a detriment, especially if those changes aren't for the better. Think about how you would feel if you expected to date Dr. Jekyll and Mr./Ms. Hyde showed up.

God tells us that He accepts us and gives us the freedom to be who we are—warts and all. (See Psalm 103:13-14.) Does that mean you have to reveal every tiny flaw to a potential date because you want to give an honest impression of yourself? No! You *can* put your best foot forward and be the best *you* you can be.

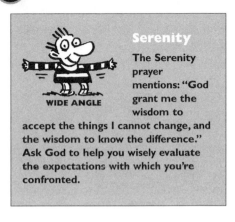

Serenity

The Serenity prayer mentions: "God grant me the wisdom to accept the things I cannot change, and the wisdom to know the difference." Ask God to help you wisely evaluate the expectations with which you're confronted.

WIDE ANGLE

EXPECTATIONS THAT CAN'T BE MET

You cannot be anyone or anything other than yourself. Ditto for your date. A person cannot meet another person's every unspoken need. If your potential date expects a "10" and expresses disappointment that you're ... an 8½, that's not your problem. If you know she barely has a sense of humor, don't expect her to laugh at your jokes. The key here is to be realistic about your expectations and to realistically respond to your date's expectations.

One way to respond is to avoid blame, particularly if the date did not go well. A response like "This whole evening was lousy because you're a jerk" won't go over well. Remember, "a gentle answer turns away wrath, but a harsh word stirs up anger" (Proverbs 15:1).

IS THERE A MIND READER IN THE HOUSE?

Keep in mind that no one is a mind reader. It isn't fair to blame someone for not meeting unspoken expectations. Some expectations need to be voiced before the date to avoid future disappointment or to reveal potential incompatibility. For example, if you expect to date only Christians, be honest beforehand. If you don't expect to always be the one to pay for dates, discuss early on in the relationship. It beats fuming all evening!

YOU'VE HAD A GREAT TIME ON YOUR DATE. NOW WHAT?

Contact Your Date to Say Thanks. Some people have followed up great dates with a phone call, a card, or flowers, just to say thanks for a great evening. You might contact your date in some way that's creative and consistent with your personality. Send a simple e-mail or a card through campus mail.

If you elect to call, consider a time frame that you can feel comfortable about. If calling the next day makes you seem too eager, wait a few days. (You might poll your friends to ask their opinion about how long you should wait.)

THE GREAT WAIT

If your date said that he or she would call within a certain time period, give him or her the benefit of the doubt. If, however, he or she does not call within that time frame, it's up to you to call or continue to wait. Some people who say they will call, or who give a vague "I'll call you sometime" don't always do so. This is not necessarily a reflection on you nor an indication that they did not enjoy the date. They might be procrastinators about calling. They might even be waiting for *you* to call. This is something you discover as it happens.

A word about ... your word. If you say you're going to call, at least *try* to call. You will avoid causing hard feelings. If you say you're going to call and don't, your date might consider your word to be unreliable. The best thing to do is to do what you said you would do.

GO ON ANOTHER DATE

The best follow-up to a good date is the assurance that there will be another one. Once you've both decided that you definitely want to see each other, you need to:

Choose a different venue. If your first date was over coffee or was basically a trial run, you might choose a restaurant, a museum, or a sporting event as a follow-up.

Examine your expectations. What are your expectations? If you go with the expectation that this date will be *better* than the previous one, you will probably be headed for a disappointment, even if the date turns out good. Take time to adjust your expectations to a realistic level before you go out with the person again. Consider also that he or has expectations as well. (See "What Did *You* Expect?" for tips on dealing with a date's expectations.)

Take time to relate, rather than worrying about a relationship. Use the time to get to know one another and have fun. Each time you get together with this person, you'll learn something more about her. A second date does not necessarily mean you're in an exclusive relationship with her. If you're worried about whether the person wants a relationship or not, you won't have much fun. More than likely, if you both enjoy each other's company and make plans for yet another date, a relationship has already developed.

EVALUATE THE EXPERIENCE

GET OVER IT

Some people fear evaluating their dates, because they fear learning the truth. *After all,* a person might think, *Bob's a great guy. The date wasn't all that I expected and he did*

Fearing the Truth

When I am afraid, I put my trust in you.
Psalm 56:3 NLT

THE BIBLE SAYS

sort of act a little dumb toward the end. But who else is there for me to date? I've got to stick with Bob, right? Or: *Sheila's pretty cool. She's certainly beautiful. Maybe she seemed a little vapid, but who cares, right?* The point is, you *do* care. And so does God. If you're afraid to evaluate an experience because (a) you *know* you're settling, (b) you don't think you have any other options, consider the message of Psalm 56:3.

Once you've come down from the "high" of a good date, it's time to evaluate. Was it really good? Was it enough to cause you to want to see the person again? Use the questions below to evaluate your experience.

1. What are your immediate impressions of this date?

2. Was there anything that happened that you particularly liked? disliked?

For each of the following questions, circle a number that fits closest to how you feel.

3. How would you rate this date?

1	2	3	4	5	6	7	8	9	10
A disaster					Good				Great

4. How much information did you learn about your date?

1	2	3	4	5	6	7	8	9	10
Next to nothing				Some things			I want to know more		

5. How much information do you think your date learned about you?

1	2	3	4	5	6	7	8	9	10
Next to nothing				Some things			I want to know more		

6. Now, think about this: how much of the real you did your date get to know?

1	2	3	4	5	6	7	8	9	10
Only my name				Some of the real me		I was as real as possible			

7. How much of your date's real personality did you get to know?

I	2	3	4	5	6	7	8	9	10

Hardly anything   Some of the real him/her   The whole nine yards

8. How did you expectations about the evening match up to reality?

I	2	3	4	5	6	7	8	9	10

They did not match   Matched to some degree   We have a match!

9. Refer back to the rating you gave this date. Why did you choose that rating?

10. Would you ask this person out/go out with this person again? Why or why not?

Prayerfully evaluate your responses. This is not an exercise to get you to obsess over every detail of the date. This is merely a tool to help you know whether you *should* see the person again. If in the light of the second day you realize you're not that excited about seeing the person, that could be an indication that maybe you shouldn't. If you don't hear from the person after a long while, that's another indication.

SECTION 6
RESPECTING YOUR DATE

RESPECTING YOUR DATE

THE BEST KEPT LOVE SECRET

Giving encouragement just may be the best kept secret to loving relationships. Think of it as the oil that keeps things running smoothly in all the
complicated parts of a relationship. A little bit of preventative maintenance
goes a long way toward a solid relationship between two people. In case you
need a tune-up in the creativity department when it comes to encouraging
your date, check out these ideas:

Wait a Minute Mr. Postman

Send your guy or girl a note in the mail…even if you live in the same apartment complex! No return address and a typed mailing label will extend the
suspense!

At the Tone…

Leave your message! At the end of a great time together, give your date a
quick voice mail message waiting for them when they get home as a surprise
reminder of your care!

Compliments of…

Everyone responds to compliments! Take time to notice something special
about that special person and say it. Sincerity is encouraging!

You've Got Mail

Having an e-mail waiting for you is like opening a present! Pass along one of those uplifting "deep thoughts" that float around the Internet or look up a positive verse from Psalms to keep their spirits up. Try delaying your message for them to receive it if you're out of town for the weekend.

CATCH A CLUE

Nice to Notice

"One of my best friends at work always has something nice to say about somebody. It's not like she's laying it on thick or whatever. It's just nice that she notices."—Brad, Atlanta, Georgia

Sweet Words

For a special occasion, give your date a message they'll not soon forget! You need a poster board, tape, marker, several candies and candy bars and a bit of creativity. Write a message to your date using the candy bars, to substitute for specific words, taping them onto the poster board at the appropriate place.

> *Example:*
> Hey Sweetheart (use a package of "SweeTarts" here)! If you ask me, you're the best in the (use a "MilkyWay" candy bar here)! And you've got that ("100,000 Dollar" bar here) smile that blows me away!

Continue your note until you run out of room or candy—whichever comes first! For more ideas, walk the candy aisle at a convenience store and see what names bring sweet thoughts to mind!

Think on This

If he's facing a major test or big job interview this week, leave a post-it note of an uplifting Bible verse on his mirror where he'll see it each day.

TREATING YOUR DATE WITH RESPECT

IF YOU WANT IT, YOU GOTTA GIVE IT

The Golden Rule of respect is: If you want it, you gotta give it. The best relationships are built on mutual respect. We can't realistically expect respect from another person without giving it ourselves. The Bible puts it this way:

> *"Be devoted to one another in brotherly love. Honor one another above yourselves."* Romans 12:10

Take this short quiz to rate your Respect-O-Meter toward others

1. Do you talk more than you listen on dates?
2. Do you find yourself criticizing the other person when you're together?
3. Do you invite the other person's opinion on topics of conversation?
4. Do you make fun of your date's choice of friends?
5. Do you tell your friends personal things about your date?
6. Do you ever stretch the truth to impress your date?

If you answered "yes" to more than one question, you may need to work on treating others more respectfully. Again, you must give respect before you can expect it from other people. It's all about putting someone else before yourself and treating others the way you would like to be treated. If you love to talk about yourself, learn to ask people questions about themselves. If you find yourself overly critical, substitute an encouraging word instead—even if finding the right word takes practice! When you make respecting others a priority, others will increase their respect toward you.

R-E-S-P-E-(-T

A disrespectful relationship is an abusive one. If a person does not respect you, that person does not deserve a date with you! No wonder Aretha Franklin was so worked up! Look at the following vital signs of a healthy, mutually respectful relationship. A man or woman who respects you will

R—Remind you of your successes and not your failures.

E—Expect the best from you and help you be your best.

S—See that your needs are met alongside their own.

P—Practice self-control sexually and emotionally.

E—Encourage you to achieve your dreams.

C—Cut you slack when you fail, not cut you with their words.

T—Take time to listen and talk when you need it.

Given these vital signs, what's the pulse of your current relationship? Remember, respect is a two-way street. No relationship can rest on one individual's effort. If it's not mutual, it's not worth it.

QUALITY AND QUANTITY TIME

QUALITY TIME VERSE QUANTITY TIME

No, this isn't another armchair psychologist books that wants to draw a one-size-fits-all conclusion to the argument of quantity time versus quality time in a relationship. The truth is, the argument differs from couple to couple, depending on what either partner views as most valuable. Some people don't care what they do together, as long as it's a chunk of time spent with the person they care about. Quantity time. Others might feel hurt if the moments aren't filled with forethought and planning down to the last second. Quality time.

Everyone speaks a different language when it comes to interpreting love and affection. Therefore, it's important to find out what side of the time issue you are on and the side of your dating partner. For example, check out these slightly exaggerated ideals:

The Quantity-Time Girl

Give this girl the time of day, several times and in several ways. Studying in the library, running errands around town, etc. She's pretty easy on how you fill her relational time slots—as long as you're together. But don't take advantage of her low-maintenance exterior either.

The Quality-Time Guy

This guy does things wholeheartedly. He's likely the busy type—but don't assume his lack of free time means a lack of interest. His aim is spending a well-purposed evening together with meaningful conversation and attention.

In the extreme, both sides have their own pitfalls to beware. However, most couples are a combination of the two pictures above. They may both be quantity-time people, quality-time junkies, or something in the middle. Either way, all healthy, mutually satisfying relationships take time, period. How, where, and why you spend time together forms the basis of your relationship. The following are areas to watch out for concerning the time-factor in your dating relationships.

"Time-Bombs" to Any Dating Relationship:

Daytimers: Do you have to call each other for an appointment to set a time to set an appointment to set a date? Everybody's busy, but no one likes feeling they're dating Franklin Quest instead. Take a serious look at your schedule and pencil in some flexibility.

Movies: When is the last time you had a meaningful and edifying conversation in the movie theater? Albeit the newest release is the most popular choice for a Friday night, at the end of the evening you've shared two hours of your life and one large popcorn but you don't know each other any better. Isn't it time to get creative?

Physical Involvement: Your parents called it "necking," but whether you're "mugging," "macking," or just plain making out, marathon kissing sessions are the cheapest dates. But watch out! If every date ends up this way, you're not only pushing the envelope sexually, you're cheapening your communication level with each other.

Routines: Relational ruts form when the ordinary becomes the inevitable. You're in a rut when each date winds up as a make-out session. You're in a rut with dinner and a movie every Friday at 7 P.M. Spark some creativity in your date-planning together and put your relationship in a new context next Friday.

A RADICAL APPROACH TO DATING

Try a radical approach to dating—practice the art of sacrificing your desires for another person in the areas that matter most to us.

OUR TIME

Run that errand for him that isn't in your daytimer schedule! Do your dates revolve around your time schedule alone?

CATCH A CLUE

Thinking of Others

"I guess dating used to be a way for me to find the right girl for me. I was always looking at how this girl or that girl made me feel. Pretty soon I realized my whole dating life was all about me—what I could get. No wonder they all ended in break ups. When I started looking at what I could give to someone else, instead of the other way around, my relationships really matured, you might say. I became a lot happier with myself and it's made me more content in my dating life."—**Kyle, Ft. Collins, Colorado**

OUR THOUGHTS

If you're in a relationship, think about ways to show her you care for her… more than you wish she would do this or that for you. If you're interested in dating someone, think about character qualities you can give toward a quality relationship more than you daydream about your own needs.

THE ROLE OF EMOTIONS

WHO'S DRIVING?

Picture this. A sleek, oh-so-shiny red convertible, poised in the driveway like lava ready to hurl itself down the side of a mountain. We're talking smooth. We're talking fast. We're talking speed-city.

Most Important

"Above all else, guard your heart, for it is the well-spring of life." (Proverbs 4:23)

THE BIBLE SAYS

Then picture the chubby hands of a fourth grade boy clenched around the steering wheel. Mud-stained fingers clumsily turn the key and whamo! Ignition! Destination: the nearest expressway!

"Wait a minute!" you say? A child driving such a machine? Are you nuts? No, just giving a picture of the wild ride we put ourselves through when we come across something as powerful as a relationship and let our emotions take the wheel. Our hearts simply do not have the maturity to handle the experience required for safe travel. Out of control and unprotected emotions put us in danger.

WHAT'S THE BEST ROLE FOR EMOTIONS IN A RELATIONSHIP?

Let's face it: We are complicated beings! Emotions like love, anger, and sadness are complex experiences that bring our existence to life like color brought to black-and-white television! Emotions find their best role enhancing a relationship. Sharing parts of ourselves in special conversations and moments with someone is one of life's greatest thrills. Emotions are created for our enjoyment. However, they can never substitute for substance between two people. Emotions make us feel all gooey inside when we feel we're in love. But it takes more than "goo" to love someone down the road—especially when you don't "feel" very loving.

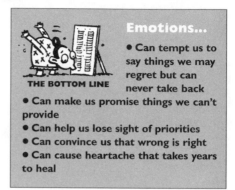

THE BOTTOM LINE

Emotions...

• **Can tempt us to say things we may regret but can never take back**
• **Can make us promise things we can't provide**
• **Can help us lose sight of priorities**
• **Can convince us that wrong is right**
• **Can cause heartache that takes years to heal**

That kind of love is based on a commitment, not a crush. Don't mistake gooey emotions of love for the "real thing." How can you tell the difference?

IS IT LOVE OR IS IT THE STOMACH FLU?

Check the "symptoms" you are feeling (a fluttery stomach, rapid heart beat) against these tried and description of true love found in 1 Corinthians 13.

❏ Love is patient.
❏ Love is kind.
❏ It does not envy.
❏ It does not boast.
❏ It is not proud.
❏ It is not rude.
❏ It is not self-seeking.
❏ It is not easily angered.
❏ It keeps no record of wrongs.
❏ Love does not delight in evil but rejoices with the truth.
❏ It always protects, always trusts, always hopes, always perseveres.
❏ Love never fails.

PROTECTING YOUR EMOTIONS

"I WANT TO GET OFF!"

Emotions are pretty powerful creations. They can take us to the highest highs and the lowest lows all on one ride—a' la a "relationship rollercoaster." So, in order to experience the thrill dating can be on a more even keel, we have to learn to control our feelings before they control us. Consider the following tips when keeping your emotions in check.

DON'T DUMP ON THE FIRST DATE

Hold off right away introducing each other to every skeleton in your closet. It may feel "bonding" to get so deep so quickly on a moonlit night. But in the light of day you or he might think twice about the revelations!

Don't Underestimate a Spiritual Bond
Talking about your inner beliefs and even praying together can be unexpectedly intimate—especially between members of the opposite sex. Be wise in your choice of "prayer partners"—it may stir up confusion and feelings neither intended.

Know Thyself
What is an emotional weakness for you? For many women, talking on an intimate level is bonding. For most men, physical intimacy is lockstep with their emotions. Be wise in situations that require an emotional investment for which you are not ready.

PROTECTING YOUR DATE'S EMOTIONS

BEING RESPONSIBLE

It's one thing to keep your own emotions in check in relation to the opposite sex. But it's equally important to take an others' feelings into consideration as well. While it might break "The Rules," becoming a master of

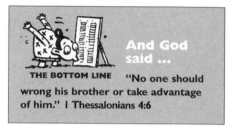

And God said ...

THE BOTTOM LINE "No one should wrong his brother or take advantage of him." I Thessalonians 4:6

manipulating others isn't the bottom line of all dating advice. It's all about becoming a responsible person of character—not just looking out for number one.

Here are some areas to keep in mind:

Say What You Mean—And mean what you say. If you sense that your date is moving ahead of your own feelings, don't encourage the rapid pace. Speak the truth in a loving, not misleading, way.

Don't Manipulate—Late nights. Moonlit roads. Secluded walks. Don't manipulate a setting for emotional or physical intimacy that your relationship isn't ready to handle.

"Missionary" Dating—Pursuing a relationship with the hopes of "changing" a person's differing major religious or moral facet runs the risk of emotional entrapment. The relentless pursuit of incompatibility is not fair to either party.

Handle With Care—A person on the "rebound" from a recent break up is especially vulnerable to new caring relationships. Be sensitive to their unique needs and be careful.

LETTING SOMEONE KNOW YOU'RE NOT INTERESTED

WATCH YOUR MOTIVE

Everyone has one. But no one's ever really seen one. You know, a motive. In the area of relationships, motives are very important. Using the right motives, relationships and friendships with others can be a mutually satisfying experience. However, sometimes we have misleading motives. They keep us from telling a person how we really feel about them. We may "keep them hanging" because we like the attention even though we may not reciprocate the other's romantic feelings. There is a temptation to use the other person for what they can "do" for us. It's a good idea to ask yourself one question whenever you are in relationship with

WOW!

Top Ten Worst Lines to Let Someone Know you're not interested

10. I have an open-book test tomorrow and I have to study.
9. I'm downloading the *Revenge of Freecell* this evening.
8. I can't go out, but my roommate is free tonight.
7. I have to wash my hair. Twice.
6. Let me check my daytimer first.
5. "And miss must-see TV?"
4. My guppies just had babies and I promised to sit for them tonight.
3. I'm three years behind in completing my scrapbook and I'm catching-up tonight.
2. My little sister's Barbie stuff is a mess and we're re-organizing Barbie's closet tonight.
1. I'm expecting an e-mail tonight, sorry.

another person: "What's my motive for being with this person?" The Bible gives us a good measuring rod for keeping our motives in check: "Love must be sincere ... honor one another above yourselves." (Romans 12:9-10)

MIXED SIGNALS

What is it about seeing that yellow signal that seems to instinctively propel our "pedal to the metal" in hopes of making it through the intersection? It's not quite a green light. But it's not quite a "stop" signal either. Interpret this signal the wrong way and the result is painful. Sending mixed signals in a relationship causes hurt, too.

Red light
If you're not interested in a dating relationship with a potential paramour, say so upfront! Red lights mean stop!

Green light
If things are going well in a friendship that has potential for more, follow the green light.

Yellow light
If a friendship is moving too quickly for you or you're not sure how you or the other person feels, don't mix your signals. If a yellow light is flashing in your head every time you're together, follow it's directions: Use caution. Slow down. Figure out how you feel and send a clear signal that says what you mean.

CREATIVE AND CHEAP WAYS TO SHOW AFFECTION

- Bake a batch of his/her favorite cookies
- Make a "mix" of favorite songs
- Send an e-mail
- Send a note in the mail
- Put a note in his/her lunch
- Leave a note on his/her car
- Prepare his/her favorite meal
- Surprise him/her with his/her favorite dessert
- Buy a favorite CD he/she's been wanting
- Purchase tickets to a concert
- Buy flowers
- Write a poem
- Dedicate a song on the radio
- Plan a picnic
- Give a framed picture of you both
- Make an album of pictures of the two of you

- Watch his/her favorite TV show or sporting event together
- Take him/her to a favorite restaurant
- Stop by at his/her work for a surprise visit
- Share an appropriate Bible verse and leave it in a special place for him/her to find it
- Do his/her laundry
- Clean his/her living place
- Make him/her a candle
- Bring doughnuts and coffee after a long night of studying
- Plan an all-day surprise date
- Invest time in people who he/she cares about—make dinner for his/her family
- Wash his/her car
- Write a message in the dust of his/her car

- Run his/her errands
- Attend his/her sporting activities
- Bring lunch/dinner when he/she is to busy to prepare something or leave to get something
- Wrap a rose in the morning paper
- Leave a special gift in each of his/her classes (a rose, chocolates, etc.)
- Bake his/her favorite pie and leave it in the refrigerator for him/her
- Scan a picture of both of you and put it as a screen saver or wallpaper on his/her computer
- Put a note in the book that he/she is reading
- Tape a note on the inside of a newspaper or magazine that he/she reads
- Leave a note in one of his/her folders/notebooks for school
- Make a collage
- Cut out a funny comic strip that shares your humor and give it to him/her
- When it snows, write a message in his/her driveway or lawn
- Serve fortune cookies and leave your own personal message inside
- Ask questions about things he/she enjoys (sports, reading, etc.)
- Prepare a meal that has a fun theme (spring, love, Italy, etc.)
- Find a magazine article that he/she would be interested in
- Design coupons to give him/her (ex. "good for one free dessert" "good for one free date to the movies")
- Write an encouraging note on things that you appreciate in him/her
- Make a creative card such as by cutting letters from a magazine or writing on the back of old wallpaper
- Write an "appointment" in his/her datebook for the two of you to have a date together
- Plan a mystery date
- Buy him/her a present
- Buy or make him/her a calendar and write special events on it for the both of you to do together
- Leave a nice message on his/her answering machine
- Make or buy a bouquet of cookies for him/her
- Fill up his/her car with heart-shaped balloons

SECTION 7
GOING DEEPER

TRANSITION INTO A DEEPER RELATIONSHIP

WHAT'S NEXT?

You've spent countless hours hanging out, had many a dinner and movie, and you really have fun together. It seems you have a lot in common, and it feels like things are really clicking between the two of you. Are you feeling ready for more of a commitment? Could it be time to take the relationship to the next level? How do you know if it's time to move the relationship a little deeper?

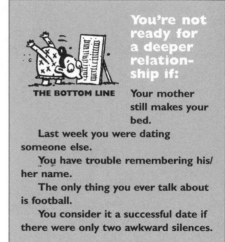

THE BOTTOM LINE

You're not ready for a deeper relationship if:

Your mother still makes your bed.

Last week you were dating someone else.

You have trouble remembering his/her name.

The only thing you ever talk about is football.

You consider it a successful date if there were only two awkward silences.

DR. JECKLE AND MR. HYDE

Hopefully up to this point in the relationship you've been yourself, but most of us tend to put our best foot forward as long as possible. However, at some point, the other person has to get to know the real you. This means they are going to see some of your "less than perfect" qualities. (Like you rarely floss your teeth.) Yes, it's possible that they could reject you, but you also might find that they still care about you. Opening yourself up is risky, but the benefits of knowing someone cares about the real you far outweigh the negatives. So go ahead—be proud of who God made you, and be yourself.

WEARING ROSE-COLORED GLASSES

If you want to grow closer to this person, the rose-colored glasses must come off for you to see them for who they really are. Your perfect picture of them will become tainted. But don't despair. No one is flawless, not even you. (I know it's hard to believe.) So don't freak out when you find out that he's organizationally challenged, or she doesn't cook like your mother. It's all part of moving deeper into the relationship.

You know you're wearing glasses if you think:
- He/she never has bad breath.
- His/her hair always looks great.
- He/she always knows the right thing to say.
- He/she can meet all your needs.
- He/she is perfect in every way.

DIVING DEEPER

The goal of transitioning into a deeper relationship is ultimately to find out if this is the person you want to marry. But the transition isn't a jump. Going deeper into a relationship is a little like scuba diving. The transition down must be slow and smooth. The pressure from jumping too quickly to the next relationship level could destroy your friendship just as plunging too quickly to a lower depth could possibly kill you. You're friends already, right? Then focus on becoming closer friends and take your time getting to know each other better. Ease into the relationship.

HAVING A HEALTHY RELATIONSHIP

TEST OF TIME

Many couples think that because they have been dating for years, they must be doing something right. But dating length of time is not an indication of relationship health. Having a healthy relationship doesn't just happen. It takes a lot of work and an ounce of prevention. So if you want to stay out of the doctor's office, practice a little relationship preventative medicine.

CATCH A CLUE

Top Five Expectations That Are Sure to Ruin Your Relationship:

Expecting that:
- She will start doing your laundry.
- He will forsake his friends to go out on a date with you every Friday and Saturday night.
- He will never again talk to any other women, except his mother.
- Serious equals the "M" word (marriage).
- Children's names must be agreed upon.

VACCINATE YOUR RELATIONSHIP

The best way to fight off disease is to communicate, communicate, communicate. And not just about your weekend plans, or what someone said to someone else. Communication is a two-way street that maintains a balance between talking and listening. If there's a problem between you, don't give the silent treatment. Nor is it wise to blow your stack and start yelling. Rather, talk it out. Share your thoughts but listen to theirs as well.

And be sure to be honest when you communicate. Lying or telling the other person what you think they want to hear is no way to build a healthy relationship.

STAYING HEALTHY

A healthy relationship maintains a balance between the mental, physical, and spiritual aspects of life. When too much time is spent in one area, the relationship takes on unhealthy characteristics.

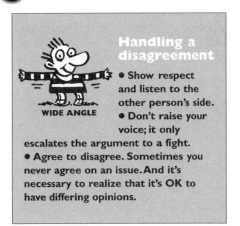

Handling a disagreement

WIDE ANGLE

● Show respect and listen to the other person's side.
● Don't raise your voice; it only escalates the argument to a fight.
● Agree to disagree. Sometimes you never agree on an issue. And it's necessary to realize that it's OK to have differing opinions.

Physical
If kissing, touching, etc. is dominating your time together, the relationship is at risk. Just like one can't survive on dessert for nourishment, a relationship can't survive strictly on physical involvement.

Mental
If you're spending too much time in the physical department, then you can bet that the mental/social aspect of your relationship is lacking.

Spiritual
Often not enough attention is given to this aspect of the relationship. But God calls us to hold each other accountable and to encourage each other to love and serve Him.

"And let us consider how we may spur one another on toward love and good deeds." (Hebrews 10:24)

MAINTAINING PRIORITIES

Priorities keep a relationship grounded and focused. They keep it on track and headed in the right direction. But it's easy to let priorities fall by the wayside when our desire to be loved takes the driver's seat.

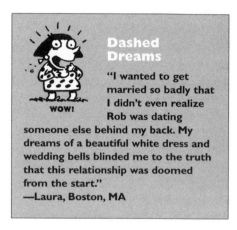

Dashed Dreams

"I wanted to get married so badly that I didn't even realize Rob was dating someone else behind my back. My dreams of a beautiful white dress and wedding bells blinded me to the truth that this relationship was doomed from the start."
—Laura, Boston, MA

GRAND ILLUSIONS

It's easy to idealize marriage. It's so romantic, and being in love feels good. Couples can get so enamored with the idea of marriage that their priorities get out of whack. Some people want to get married so much that the hint of getting serious sends them running to the wedding dress or tuxedo store before they even know their date's middle name. Since the goal is not to gain a mate at any cost, don't send the relationship into overdrive just because you can't wait to walk down the aisle. Make it a priority to really get to know your date, rather than speed through this phase in your relationship.

WHAT'S IMPORTANT?

Certainly there will be issues which you feel strongly about, some you'll be willing to compromise on, and some you'll not. Make it a priority in your relationship to talk about these issues and those that are important to your date. For instance, maybe it's important to you that a woman stay home with the family rather than work. Because your date may have differing ideas about this issue, it should be a priority to discuss.

ISSUES TO DISCUSS

- Does your idea of a family include a pet or does the thought of an animal in the house make you gag (or sneeze)?
- Do you organize your sock drawer by color or are you lucky to find a pair anywhere in your room?
- Is your idea of a vacation bungee jumping or antiquing?
- Is your idea of exercise training for a 10K race or walking to the refrigerator?
- Do you spend money extravagantly or do you get to the restaurant for the early bird special and have a half-price coupon in hand?

WHO'S FIRST?

Couples can get so head over heels in love with each other that God gets pushed out of the picture. But seeking God should be a priority in your life and in your relationship. How do we make God a priority, you ask?
- Study the Bible
- Pray to God
- Honor God with your life and dating

PACING YOUR DATES

S-L-O-W

Ever ride a roller coaster? The thrill is in the speed of the turns, the ups, the downs, the surprises ahead. But try riding an intense roller coaster two or three times in a row, and you may be looking for the nearest exit. Your head is spinning, your stomach is churning, and your lunch is about to pay you another visit.

Dating can be a lot like that. A new dating relationship is both exciting and thrilling. It'll send you to emotional highs because you'll anticipate everything that's coming. But if you let yourself ride that roller coaster too much, you may find yourself wanting out—*fast*.

Most couples *rush* into dating. They get too serious *too* fast. The result is heartbreak, disappointment. They rush themselves in many ways.

DON'T FORGET

Use Your Limits

You have limits. You have a physical and emotional intimacy you want to share one day with only your spouse. You have a mental commitment you want to reserve only for him or for her. Keep those in mind. You don't want to get to your limit early on in the relationship and have nowhere to go, except compromise. You don't want to be ABM—All But Married—in any area (especially if you don't know that this person is the one).

Keep control of yourself. You'll be tempted to give in emotionally and mentally just as much as you'll be tempted to push yourself physically. Be smart and exercise caution.

Physically

They're quick to hold hands and kiss. They reach their physical limit early in the relationship. They spend the next months or years trying to resist the temptation to go further. Or, if they've gone too far, they may carry guilt with them the rest of their lives.

Emotionally

They're quick to "feel" intimate. The bond between their hearts grows too quickly. They feel emotionally attached after a few dates or a few months. The closer they grow, the more their heart is ripped apart if things don't work out.

Mentally

They quickly decide that this is *the one*. They make plans for a year from now. They plan weddings, families, and kids. They don't plan for the disappointment they feel if it turns out this "isn't the one."

Spiritually

Because they're both Christians, they decide they want to grow spiritually, too. They spend lots of

CATCH A CLUE

How did you pace your dates?

"We started training for triathlons together. Working out was a fun and inexpensive way to see each other every day, plus we got in shape! We still compete now that we're married."—Mark, Wheaton, Illinois

"I love photography, so while we were dating, Lisa and I would go on shooting sprees—pictures that is. Together we'd go out and take pictures and then develop the film. Now that we're married, I'm a freelance photographer, and she helps me with photo shoots."—Jim, Overland Park, Kansas

"We did a lot of group dating. It was a great way to be together and still be with our friends. After three years of marriage, we still hang out with those friends."—Becky, Minneapolis, Minnesota

time reading the Bible together and lots of time praying together. This is often a good thing. The problem is that our emotions and spiritual life are closely related. A carefree jump into the spiritual realm seems good, but can also lead to heartache.

YOU KNOW THE ATTRACTION IS PURELY PHYSICAL WHEN:

- You look at her and all you see is a vision of beauty with long flowing hair.
- Every date is spent in a lip lock.
- His picture is plastered everywhere in your room.
- You know nothing about her even though you've been dating for months.
- You constantly daydream about his incredible body and good looks.

MAIN ATTRACTION

You're obviously physically attracted to each other or you probably wouldn't have gone out in the first place. Hopefully your relationship has moved far beyond the physical attraction in the examples listed above. As you're probably finding out, the more serious the relationship becomes, the harder it is to hold back physically. Many couples find that the longer they date, the more time they spend alone which only increases the temptation to move past God's boundaries of sexual purity. But pacing your dates can help you resist the temptation to go too far.

Don't forget, the Bible says: *"But when you are tempted, he will also provide a way out so that you can stand up under it."* (1 Corinthians 10:13)

COMMON INTERESTS

Pacing your dates takes some creativity. Step back and take a look at your common interests. Is there a hobby you can share? Maybe try something new together. Whether it's golfing, working out, or horseback riding, try to find at least one activity you like to do together. By participating in something your date enjoys, you observe him doing something he is passionate about. If it's something new for her, you will get to see how she adapts to new and different experiences. Either way, your view of her will become expanded, and your friendship will grow.

IDEAS FOR PACING YOUR DATES

Group date. If you've been group dating, then you know how much fun it can be. If you haven't, call some friends and try out the ideas from the chapter "Group Dating."

Double date with different couples. If you're a couple that doesn't have a big group of friends to hang out with, maybe you know another couple you'd like to get to know better. Double dating adds a new dimension to the exclusive date.

Periodically pick a new activity to do together.
- Volunteer at the humane society.
- Visit an elderly person at a nursing home.
- Learn how to ballroom dance.
- Play tennis or ping pong.
- Try new restaurants.
- Check out the cultural events in your town.

The ideas are endless when you decide to move past the basic dinner and a movie date. These activities will broaden your perspective about this person as you see how he handles himself in different situations. Pacing your dates slows the relationship down and takes the pressure off of getting too serious too quickly.

HAVING THE RELATIONSHIP DEFINING TALK

SWEATING BULLETS

Your heart is beating a thousand times a minute. Your palms start to sweat. Your mouth goes dry despite the gum you're frantically chewing. A million times you've practiced what you'll say, but then, doubts flood your mind. What if he isn't ready for a deeper relationship? What if this isn't the right time to talk? What if I read the signals all wrong? Even if you are best friends, and you're pretty sure he feels the same way about you as you do about him, you *still* don't know exactly what he is thinking about the relationship until you have "the talk."

Top 10 Worst Opening Lines for "The Talk"

WOW!

10. You light up my life.
9. We're like two peas in a pod.
8. God told me we should be together.
7. Wanna Tic-Tac?
6. This is the beginning of a beautiful friendship.
5. You complete me.
4. Can we get on with this?
3. My biological clock is ticking, so …
2. You remind me of my mother.
1. Well uh, uhm, hmm …

RISKY BUSINESS

Putting yourself on the line and having the talk is risky. You do face the chance of being rejected. But that risk can be minimized. Like scuba diving, you must plan and prepare before you take the plunge. In a relationship, the groundwork must be laid by spending time together and getting to know each other. Rushing into it on an emotional whim will only jeopardize the relationship. Check where you fall on the line below.

Sometimes I feel awkward around him/her	There's still some things I can't share	I can tell him/her anything

If you fall toward the left of this spectrum, it would be wise to spend more time getting to know this person before having the talk.

PRESSURE POINTS

Maybe you feel ready to take the next step in the relationship, but the other person just wants to keep dating. It could be tempting to slap him or her with an ultimatum: "If you don't want to move forward in this relationship, then I'm breaking up."

If this sounds familiar, then take a step back and examine the relationship. Have you discussed why she does not want to move forward in the relationship? Have you examined why you are in such a rush? What is your reasoning for pushing her to make a decision? Pressing someone to make a decision before they are ready will handicap your relationship and create hard feelings. If this situation arises, the relationship-defining talk may become an ongoing discussion that merits some time and attention before moving forward. But you want to be sure that both of you are in agreement rather than one person being pressured into something she's not ready for yet.

WHEN YOU SHOULD GET OUT OF A RELATIONSHIP

THE BREAK UP

It's never a pretty word, or a nice experience. What to say, how to act, when to do the deed—all these must be considered. There are legitimate reasons for breaking up and then there are not so legitimate ones.

Don't think that because you've been dating for eons, or the wedding invitations are in the mail, that there is no way out of a relationship. There are valid reasons for getting out of the relationship.

WOW!

Top five wimpy reasons to break up:

5. She got a haircut you don't like.
4. She doesn't know how to cook.
3. His family is just plain weird.
2. She bites her nails.
1. You found out he has a foot-odor problem.

NO COMPROMISE

If you're having second thoughts because there is an unresolved issue between you, then don't just continue on and hope that it goes away. If the two of you are at opposite sides of the spectrum on an important issue, and it is one you refuse to compromise on, don't sweep it under the table and pretend it doesn't really exist just because everything else is going great. The issue won't go away. And it can actually come back to haunt you.

QUICK CHANGE

If this person does not hold your same values, she most likely never will. And don't fool yourself into thinking you can change her. Rather than dating someone you are trying to make over, look for someone who has the qualities you desire and values you uphold.

GET OUT NOW!

Pay Attention

CATCH A CLUE

"John and I had been dating for several years and had talked about getting married in the near future. But one thing always bothered me. He gambled quite a bit. He said that he would quit for me, and did for awhile, but then he started again. I tried to ignore that but deep down it bothered me because I cared for him so much. Plus, I didn't want to start the whole relationship-thing over again with someone else. So we married, and now it's our biggest source of fights. If I had it to do over again, I might not have married him."
—Name withheld, Oregon

Unfortunately some people stay in a relationship because they figure it's better to be in a bad relationship then in no relationship at all. But some actions are unacceptable, and it is better to be alone than to continue on if your date is doing the following:

Abusing you either verbally or physically. No matter what your reasoning for staying in the relationship thus far, there is no need to endanger yourself, because it will likely not improve with time. Put an end to the relationship immediately and move on.

Pressuring you in any way. Whether it's for sex, money, or to get married. Be careful because pressure can be subtle. If you hear the words, "If you love me, you'll … " or even if they're implied, bid this person farewell and look elsewhere.

Controlling you. If this person is demanding that you spend all your free time with him, gets extremely upset if you're spending time with the opposite sex, or tries to tell you what to do, he could have a control problem. If you sense in any way that he is trying to control you, say sianara.

IT'S NEVER TOO LATE

If you are having any second thoughts or something is just not sitting right with you, then take some time away from the relationship. And remember, it's never too late to get out, even if it's your wedding day. It's better to call all the guests and tell them not to come than to go through with a marriage you aren't sure about.

MEETING FAMILY AND FRIENDS

BREAKING THE ICE

Because the folks you are meeting could be potential in-laws, you want to start out on the right foot with them. To help ensure that you start out in their good graces, be sure to avoid some common faux-pas.

True Story

"Wayne and I had been dating for awhile when he invited me over for dinner to meet his family.

WOW!

About halfway through the meal someone told a funny story, and when I laughed, I choked on my food and then actually threw up on the table! It was so embarrassing! But now that they are my in-laws, it's something we look back on and laugh about."
—**Kathy, Ohio**

FIVE FAUX-PAS TO AVOID

1. Sharing an embarrassing story about the other person.
2. Burping out loud (unless they are French).
3. Picking your nose while sitting at the dinner table.
4. Forgetting to zip up your pants after using the facilities.
5. Cooking shellfish only to find out they are allergic when they sit down to eat.

Meeting your date's parents and family can be a nerve-wracking experience. You want them to like you. You want to impress them. You want to make sure you don't say anything dumb. The result? You get so nervous that you don't enjoy yourself or you actually *do* say something dumb. So before the big get-together, take a few tips from the Nerve Calmers section below.

NERVE CALMERS

Before the meeting, talk to your date and learn as much as you can about his parents and family. Find out their hobbies, interests, activities, likes, and dislikes.

- Think of questions to ask and topics to discuss ahead of time.
- Share how you're feeling with your date. Sometimes when anxieties are verbalized, they don't seem so threatening.
- Consider that these people are probably nervous as well, and feeling the same way you are.
- Take a deep breath, hold it for 10 seconds and then s-l-o-w-l-y blow it out. Do this three times to slow down your beating heart.

HELPFUL HINTS

Now that you've calmed your nerves and are ready to meet the family, take a few steps to ensure that the pow-wow goes smoothly.

- Be yourself
- Be courteous
- Be respectful

BIBLICAL GUIDELINES FOR LOVE AND MARRIAGE

We all have our own ideas about what love is. But they can get pretty warped if we base them on society's view of love. If you want to know what real love looks like, take a peek in the Bible.

WHAT DOES THE BIBLE SAY ABOUT LOVE?

It's pretty well spelled out for us in 1 Corinthians 13, also known as the "Love Chapter":

> "Love is patient, love is kind. It does not envy, it does not boast, it is not proud. It is not rude, it is not self-seeking, it is not easily angered, it keeps no record of wrongs. Love does not delight in evil but rejoices with the truth. It always protects, always trusts, always hopes, always perseveres. Love never fails." (1 Corinthians 13:4-8)

Whew! Those are some high standards! Granted, this is *perfect* love—an example of how God loves us, but it is the kind of love we should strive to give in our own relationships.

TAKE IT SERIOUSLY

Marriage is truly a wonderful institution. But it should not be taken lightly. It is a sacred covenant before God and should be honored and respected. *Marriage should be honored by all.* (Hebrews 13:4)

CHRISTIANS NEED TO MARRY CHRISTIANS

The Bible is very clear about who and whom we shouldn't marry. While it's not going to flat out tell you if who you're dating is or is not the one for you, it does command that we not marry a unbeliever. This union can weaken your Christian commitment, integrity and standards. On this, the Bible says: "Do not be yoked together with unbelievers." (2 Corinthians 6:14)

STAY COMMITTED

The Bible is also very clear about adultery. Basically it all boils down to the fact that it's not an option. So if you are unsure about this person and your eyes tend to wander, consider slowing down and taking time to really consider if he is who you want to marry. Because once the vows have been said and the cake has been cut, even looking at another person lustfully is considered adultery. (See Exodus 20:14; Matthew 5:28)

NOT QUICK TO DIVORCE

In today's society divorce is a very common and acceptable answer to marital problems. Statistics show the divorce rate soaring as people jump from one marriage to the next. But what is not shown on the charts is the deep sense of anger, pain, and bitterness left in the wake of those broken marriages. God intended that we marry only one person, so be very careful in your decision-making process.

"To the married I give this command (not I, but the Lord): A wife must not separate from her husband … And a husband must not divorce his wife." (1 Corinthians 7:10-11)

SECTION 8
WHEN IT DOESN'T WORK OUT

ENDING A BAD DATE

"You win some, you lose some."

"Nobody bats 1.000."

"Into every life a little rain must fall."

Say it however you want, but the truth is you will eventually find yourself on a bad date. What's that? It could be the result of a million and one things. But usually it's a situation where things just don't work out. Your personali-

WOW!

Top Ten Signs You May Be on a Bad Date with the Wrong Person

10. When you pick her up she says, "Could we kind of hurry out to the car? I really would rather my neighbors NOT see me with you!"

9. He keeps saying, "You're really fun, Jennifer!" ... but your name is Courtney.

8. Midway through the movie she leans over and whispers, "So, do you have any cute friends?"

7. When he shows up to get you, *his* dress clashes with your outfit.

6. On the way home from dinner, he says, "Tell me your name again?"

5. He tries to help you off the subway train ... but it's still going 20 mph!

4. When the restaurant hostess asks how many are in your party, you say "Two" and your date quickly interjects, "Better make that one!"

3. You ask him, "Where are we going?" and he replies, "Someplace really dark and loud, so I don't have to look at you or listen to you."

2. As you climb into his car, he snarls, "Let's hurry up and get this over with!"

1. After you give your order to the waiter, she says, "Can you make mine 'to go.' "

ties don't connect. Or they clash! Either there's no "chemistry" whatsoever or there's a volatile reaction in the lab of your emotions. To put it nicely, you want to tell the other person, "Have a nice life" and go home. How do you end a bad date?

REMARKS THAT CAN GET YOU HOME EARLY

"Even though I'm having a *really* fun time, I probably ought to go check on my family. It's so strange! The doctors *still* don't know where we all picked that Ebola virus!"

"You know, Steve, I just remembered my dad, for some strange reason, can't stand guys with the name Steve. It would be most unfortunate if he did to *you* what he did to the last Steve I dated."

"I don't tell this to just everybody, but my goal is to one day become a monk/nun."

"Does death fascinate you the way it does me? I just think it would be *so awesome* to study medicine and then get to do what Dr. Kevorkian does!"

"After a lot of study I'm convinced the Shakers were right about sex being sinful. It's wrong even between married couples!"

BEHAVIOR THAT CAN GET YOU HOME EARLY

- Intentionally dump a drink on yourself
- Cry hysterically while screaming "Mommy!" over and over
- Vomit
- Start yodeling at the top of your lungs during dinner
- Threaten to jump out of the car
- Announce you'd like to go get matching tattoos on your foreheads
- Reveal that you'd REALLY enjoy spending the evening driving around and running over small animals

THE RIGHT WAY TO END A BAD DATE

Be Mature
Don't judge on mere externals. Deciding a date is "bad" because his nose is bigger than you realized, or she's a little on the heavy side is immature and says more about you than it does about the other person. Go against the flow of culture and look beneath the surface for all the good and unique stuff that God put in that person.

Be Wise
Don't rush to judgment. A lot of happily married folks had terrible first dates. Millions of friendships had rocky beginnings. It just took a while for them to "connect."

Be Prayerful
Before you "burn a bridge," ask God to help you see his purpose and plan. You'll need His strength to do the right thing the right way.

Be Honest
Yes, most people lie, or shade the truth, but that doesn't mean you need to follow suit. Have some integrity. Be above board. If things aren't working out "romantically," say so; however …

Be Gentle
Consider the other person's feelings. The Bible says we need to speak the truth in love (Ephesians 4:15). The famous Golden Rule (Luke 6:31) urges us to treat others the same way we want to be treated.

Be Tactful
Stick to the issue, which is "dating." Don't be insensitive and resort to callous criticism or personal attack.

REASONS FOR BREAKING UP

WHEN THE COUPLE IS AT ODDS SPIRITUALLY

Many couples relate only on an emotional level and/or on the physical plane. They don't realize that it's possible to connect also on a spiritual level.

How so?

The Bible makes it clear that we come into this world spiritually dead (Ephesians 2:1) and separated from the life of God (Ephesians 4:18). It's when we put our faith in Christ (John 5:24) that we are "born again" (John 3:3) spiritually. At that very moment, the eternal life of God floods our souls and we become truly alive (Colossians 2:12-13). Suddenly we have the ability to relate to other "spiritually alive" people at a deepest level.

Oil and Water?

Ham and eggs. Salt and pepper. Peanut butter and jelly. Some couples are made for each other. But others—oil and water, matches and gasoline—just don't go together.

You can see the potential for problems, then, when a believer in Christ ends up dating an unbeliever. While they may have a good time together and care deeply for one another, their relationship has no spiritual base. They are not in sync at the deepest level.

It's for this reason that Paul urged the Christians in Corinth NOT to enter deep relationships with non-Christians (see 2 Corinthians 6:14-15).

Churches (and counselors' offices) are filled with sad people who did not heed this biblical command. Because they didn't end a relationship at an early stage, they now have tremendous heartache and regret. Which is worse? A dating break up or a broken life?

WHEN HE AND SHE ARE TOO DIFFERENT PERSONALLY

While there is some truth to the old saying that "Opposites attract!" it is also true that personality differences can eventually become the source of tremendous conflict. Endearing and unique traits often end up being annoying and irritating quirks that cause couples to scream and shout or smolder and pout. This explains why so many married couples endure rather than enjoy one another. For all practical purposes they are roommates and not soulmates.

WIDE ANGLE

Tough Stuff

Neil Sedaka: "Breaking up is hard, so hard to do."

If you find yourself being outwardly (or even inwardly) critical of your "sweetheart's" taste in music, hobbies, clothes, etc., it may be a good sign that you're not a good match. Dating is the best time to gather these kinds of facts.

WHEN THE RELATIONSHIP IS PHYSICALLY OUT OF CONTROL

How many couples have a relationship that is based almost entirely on physical affection? Way too many! Take away the sensual involvement and there's not much left. Over time (believe it or not!) even sex, if that's all there is, can become dull and monotonous and leave participants feeling empty and alone.

A relationship without a solid emotional and, most importantly, spiritual foundation is a dead-end street. If you're dating someone who's interested only in your body, that's a warning signal to get out!

WHEN THE RELATIONSHIP IS EMOTIONALLY UNHEALTHY

You've probably seen some couples who act like they can't function apart from one another. They feel the need to be together every moment, and it's obvious to all that they are excessively dependent on one another. Someone once described a relationship like this as "two ticks in need of a dog."

The chief problem here is that the participants typically isolate themselves from most other relationships and look to each other, mere humans, to meet deep needs that only an infinite God can meet. The typical sad result is a relationship that, sooner or later, implodes. It can't take the pressure.

The truth is, people who are extremely "needy" and who tend to lean unhealthily on others are not ready for a dating relationship. Dating is not about finding someone who will take care of me (or at least it shouldn't be!); we honor God when we move toward people to serve and give and bless.

AFTER A BREAK UP

WHAT NEXT?

Dave Barry, the wise and witty syndicated columnist, has written these words:

> "For several centuries marriages were arranged by the parents, based on such things as how much cattle the bride and the groom would each bring to the union. Often the young couple wouldn't even meet until the wedding, and sometimes they were not strongly attracted to each other. Sometimes, quite frankly, they [were actually more attracted to] the cattle. So now we feel that dating is probably a better system."

A better system? Maybe. But dating still sometimes blows up in our faces. Even when we get to choose our dates, relational break ups occur.

TEMPTATIONS TO LOOK OUT FOR FOLLOWING A BREAK UP

- Running away to join the circus
- Swearing off the opposite sex
- Going in your room and refusing to come out until you're 40
- Watching TV nonstop until your brain finally turns into a putty-like substance that starts oozing out of your pores
- Eating six-and-a-half containers of ice cream
- Burning all your pictures
- Doing something crazy or unusual with your hair

- Punching holes through your closet door
- Kicking the dog
- Throwing objects through the window or TV screen
- Throwing the dog through the TV screen!

WHAT'S THE RIGHT RESPONSE AFTER A BREAK UP?

Pray ... a lot!
The truth? Oftentimes prayer does *not* change our situation, but it can and does change our perspective.

Be honest
Don't "stuff" your feelings, or put on a mask and pretend nothing's wrong. It's okay to be down. It's not a good idea to lie and deny anything is wrong.

Find a mature friend
Having a wise person in our lives is just plain smart. Such a one gives us a safe, private place to "vent." They can be a good sounding board and a check on our emotions.

Develop a plan
If you are too passive and just sit back reacting to life, the chances are greater you'll become depressed. Be proactive. Set some positive goals. Give yourself something to work towards.

Resist the urge to be petty
When we're mad, or our feelings/pride have been hurt, it's very *natural* to want to lash out. Don't!

Determine to honor God
If you claim to be a Christian, this is your great privilege in life.

AVOIDING THE REBOUND

WHAT'S A "REBOUND" RELATIONSHIP?

That's easier to describe than define. Here's a case in point:

> Tiffany is dating Hunter. They've been going together for a couple of months, but the word on the street is that the relationship is rocky. A break up is imminent. Sure enough it happens on a Friday night. By Tuesday at lunch, Tiffany has a new boyfriend.

That's a rebound relationship, bouncing from one sweetheart straight into the arms of another.

WHY ARE "REBOUNDS" UNWISE?

We may end up using others. Instead of thinking unselfishly ("I'd like to get to know this person, and serve and encourage him/her spiritually"), "rebounding" into a new relationship is usually motivated by self-centeredness ("I need someone to care for *me*, to be with *me*, to make sure *I'm* not alone").

We may end up being used! Be wary of entering a relationship with someone who has just exited another. In fact, don't do that! You'll likely end up being boyfriend/girlfriend #15 for that year, a brief stop on the way to the next conquest.

We may end up being jerks. Following a break up, our hearts are usually wounded; consequently we're not really being our best emotional selves. What does this mean? Jumping into another relationship before our hearts have properly healed may prompt us to do mean or irrational things. Consequently that new "sweetheart" ends up shaking her head and muttering, "He's a head case!" or "What a selfish pig!"

TWO OPTIONS TO "REBOUNDING"

1. Declare a moratorium.

Prescribe a self-imposed restriction on your dating life. Give yourself two or three months, minimum. Contrary to popular belief, you won't die. And guess what? If there is someone out there who wants to get to know you, REALLY wants to date you, your unavailability, rather than turning them off, will just make you that much more appealing (see the story of Jacob & Rachel in Genesis).

WOW!

A Personal Testimony

When I was a junior at a large state university, I met a Christian girl who was a member of the most popular and prestigious sorority on campus. She was also a beautiful cheerleader. I subconsciously thought that if I could date this young woman, it would prove to the worlds beyond a shadow of a doubt that I had worth, that I was somebody.

Well, guess what? She did become my girlfriend. We dated off and on for several years, but as wonderful as this woman was, she could not meet my deep needs for acceptance, love, and fulfillment. It took me several years to realize that only Jesus Christ is able to give me what I really crave most. Over time I realized I had made this girl an idol. I had centered my life around her, instead of around Christ. I trusted her to make me feel good about myself, about life, about everything—instead of looking to Christ. No human can do these things.... In short, my own insecurity doomed the relationship from the start.—Kyle, Pueblo, CO

2. Wait on God.

Rather than trying to make something good happen, trust God to make something great happen—in His perfect timing. Our culture hates to wait. Few four-letter words are considered as obscene as W-A-I-T. Who wants to do that?! This generation is into immediate gratification. Grab whatever you want and do it NOW! Otherwise you might be left with nothing.

However, don't forget, timing is everything. Great comics have it. They know if they deliver the punchline too quickly, the joke will be ruined. Successful stockbrokers have it. Selling or buying stocks at the wrong moment can be financially devastating. The best chefs have it. Adding certain spices or removing a dish from the oven at just the right instant is the key to great cooking. In the same way, knowing when to enter a relationship is an art form. And God can give us the wisdom we need to know exactly when to move (James 1:5).

HALT!

The H.A.L.T. principle says: Never make any decisions when you are *Hungry, Angry, Lonely,* or *Tired.* Most people who just broke up are at least angry and lonely. And if they fought through dinner and late into the night—as is so common during the typical break up—they probably are also hungry and tired.

CATCH A CLUE

OVERCOMING PROBLEMS

THE RIGHT APPROACH

The beginning of any new relationship is usually wonderful: special times together, warm feelings, happy memories, and a hopeful sense about the future.

Unfortunately, every new fairy tale romance is on a crash course with reality. At some point (usually sooner rather than later), problems *will* arise. That's just part of what it means to be a fallen creature in a fallen world.

ANSWERS TO THE BIGGEST PROBLEMS

1. Money.

The best and wisest course of action is to talk. Discuss the pluses and minuses of the financial examples you've had. Dialogue about your financial goals in life. Analyze your current habits of saving, spending, and giving. Get an adult you trust to recommend a basic book on personal finance that you can work through together.

2. Sex

Here the problems can be legion! Too much emphasis on touching, groping, kissing, etc., can stunt the relationship emotionally, spiritually, even conversationally. Going too far physically can introduce guilt and shame into this relationship—and also (THIS IS CRITICALLY IMPORTANT!) into all future relationships. A lot of married couples have *big* problems relating sexually because the individuals in that relationship had multiple sexual partners during their dating years.

3. Religion
Interfaith relationships (i.e., she's Christian; he's Hindu), seldom work. That's because our spiritual beliefs go to the very core of who we are. Think about it. If you are trying to follow Christ passionately, but your "sweetheart" could care less about God, or thinks he is God, suddenly you've ruled out the most important aspect of life as a topic for discussion and as a goal to pursue together. Even interdenominational (i.e., he's Catholic; she's Baptist), relationships will have troubles, depending on how different the belief systems are. It's best and wisest to find someone who closely mirrors your own spiritual convictions. Only a foolish believer gets "hooked up" with someone who doesn't share beliefs (2 Corinthians 6:14).

4. Differing backgrounds/cultures
These kinds of relationships can and do work, but those who pursue them need to understand going in that special problems and obstacles will arise. Oftentimes these couples face family and/or societal opposition.

5. Family
Shakespeare's tale of young lovers from warring families (i.e., Romeo and Juliet) is not just an interesting story to discuss in English Lit. class. Sadly, it's often an accurate picture of what happens in dating relationships. What can you do if your family is not impressed with her "to die for" blue eyes? Or if his parents don't appreciate your unique sense of humor?

The answer is "not much." You can pray. You can try to demonstrate that your relationship is healthy and God-honoring (assuming, of course, that it is!). But, ultimately, if one or both families don't approve, you face a hard, uphill battle. And (though we seldom like to admit it) it just may be that God is using your family's concerns to warn you that a certain relationship may not be such a good idea after all.

SECTION 9

IS THIS THE ONE?

THINKING OF THE FUTURE

THE DOWNSIDE

Go out with someone once or twice, and it's generally no big deal. But by the third and fourth dates, strange things begin to happen. The heart puts the emotions on high alert. The mind goes into overdrive cranking out fantasies. And the inevitable question that begins to bounce around in our brains nonstop is *"Is this the one?"*

Hey, with so many cultural expectations and so much pressure from friends, it's difficult to not start thinking about wedding bells. But, as with anything else, we need to be careful. There's a downside to becoming preoccupied with the prospect of marriage.

WOW!

Great Quotes

"One of the reasons people get married is suntan lotion; you're going to need help. There are parts of your back that you simply can't get to by yourself, and quite frankly, no one is going to do it for you who isn't married to you."—Paul Reiser, in *Couplehood*

"There's something really great about waking up and knowing somebody loves you and that you love somebody. I know that sounds gooey, but it's true. Plus you always have a date for New Year's Eve."—Billy Crystal, quoted in *Marriage Partnership* magazine

Danger #1: Missing Your Life
Many people spend so much time and energy focusing on "what might

happen" they miss out on "what actually is." By living in the future, they're not mentally and emotionally here for the present. It sounds trite, but there's a great deal of wisdom in "seizing the day" and living in the moment. Let God guide the relationship however He sees fit. Our part is simply to enjoy the process of getting to know someone.

Danger #2: Great Expectations

If your one and only hope is to find a spouse, then anything short of that will be disappointing, perhaps even devastating. Think about it. If marriage is your sole goal in dating, then it follows that you'll be disappointed in every single dating relationship in life, except maybe one—the one that ends up at the altar.

Things Mistaken for Love

A list by Christian professor, speaker, and author Howard Hendricks:

CATCH A CLUE

- Admiration
- Desire for security
- Physical attraction
- Desire to escape
- Loneliness
- Common interests
- Infatuation
- Pity
- Parental substitution
- Puppy love
- Love on the rebound

There's a better way. First Corinthians 13 says, "Love ... hopes all things." Did you catch that? Love doesn't just hope for "one thing" (i.e., marriage), it's open to "all things." By being open to whatever God might have in mind—good friendships, helpful brother-sister type relationships—you never come away sad and/or mad. So what if she doesn't end up being "the one"?! You haven't lost anything! If she ends up being a good friend, you've gained something wonderful!

PREPARING FOR MARRIAGE

BEYOND I DO

Isn't it ironic that lovestruck couples will spend megabucks and tons of energy preparing for a *wedding ceremony* that usually lasts 30 minutes, but almost no effort preparing for a *marriage relationship* that is intended to last a lifetime?

What practical things can you do to be ready one day to say "I do"?

THINGS NOT TO DO TO PREPARE FOR MARRIAGE

1. Obsess over getting married.
Make marriage your highest goal, spend hours poring over every issue of your subscription to *Modern Bride* or *Grooms Illustrated*, stare at every person you meet and mentally ask, "Is this the one?"

Those who live this way are largely miserable. And marriage continues to elude most of them.

2. Put your life on hold.
Operate with the philosophy that life won't really begin for you until you're wearing a wedding ring. Just kind of sit there waiting for "Mr. or Ms. Right" to show up in your life. Turn down opportunities to serve God out of fear that you might miss "the one."

Those who live this way are largely miserable. And marriage continues to elude most of them.

3. Be an overeager "claw" person.

A "claw" person is a guy or girl who obviously wants nothing more than to sink her claws into a mate. She's on the prowl, hunting feverishly, with that desperate look about her. In her frantic quest to snag a spouse, folks like this end up driving everyone away.

4. Demand that God provide you with a mate.

Serve God so that He will be "obligated" to give you a spouse. Instead of a "whatever" attitude that trusts and obeys God, adopt an attitude that says, "Here's MY agenda God, and you'd BETTER meet my demands!"

Those who live this way are largely miserable. And marriage continues to elude most of them. (The sovereign God does not feel obligated, even in the least, to cater to our whims. He is good (Psalm 34:8), and longs to bless us (Psalm 84:11 NLT), but not until we first surrender to His will.)

5. Settle for a mediocre walk with God.

You can exercise hours every week and have a great body. You can be making (and even saving) the big bucks in a prestigious job. But those things have very little to do with finding a mate with whom you can build a fulfilling marriage.

Those who live this way are largely miserable. And a quality marriage continues to elude most of them.

The best marriages in the world all begin with individuals who love God with all their hearts, souls, and minds. We're not talking here about mere church involvement, but about making Christ supreme in every area of one's life (Colossians 1). When this happens, relationships soar! When this commitment is absent, relationships struggle (and often sink)!

THINGS YOU CAN DO TO PREPARE FOR MARRIAGE

Learn about the purposes for marriage.
Marriage is intended to be a covenant partnership (Genesis 2) in which we give the world a stunning picture of the kind of intimacy Christ longs to have with his church (Ephesians 5). Marriage is not primarily about sex, or "my needs," or about setting up a household together. Rather, it's all about the glory of God—serving Him together.

Learn to commit.
If you have problems making and keeping commitments to a church, to a job, or to a friendship, you're *certainly* not ready to make lifelong marital vows.

Learn to be unselfish.
Remember those incredibly polite cartoon chipmunks, Chip and Dale? Whenever they came to a doorway, they'd almost argue: "After you!" "No, after you!" That's the kind of unselfishness that makes for an awesome marriage. How about you? Do you routinely put the needs of others first (Philippians 2)? Or is your natural tendency to think only of number one?

Learn to be a servant.
Christ came, not to be served, but to serve (Mark 10:45). The best marriage partners constantly try to outdo one another in this area. Good marriages are composed of givers, not takers.

Learn to communicate.
If you can't (actually the more accurate word is "won't") express what you're thinking and feeling, please, please, please, DO NOT GET MARRIED!!!! You will only succeed in making someone else extremely miserable. Find a friend,

or a trusted roommate and learn to communicate *now*—on this side of the altar. A refusal to do this is a guarantee of marital failure.

Learn to resolve conflict.
Every marriage has its own troubles. Every couple (no matter how deeply in love they may be) will disagree—often sharply. The art of living together as man and wife for life depends on your ability to work through a conflict. Again, you need to learn this skill now, with parents, friends, roommates, colleagues, and boyfriends/girlfriends. If you can't resolve conflict in these relationships as a single, you won't be able to do so later in marriage. And if you're thinking this ability is somehow granted magically to a couple by virtue of their going through an elaborate wedding ceremony, fugeddaboutit! You're in dream land!

Learn to forgive.
Billy Graham's wife said it best, "A good marriage is the union of two forgivers." What does this mean? If you're a grudge-holder and bitter person, you're not ready to tie the knot.

IS THIS THE PERSON FOR YOU?

EVEN THIS QUESTION IS CONTROVERSIAL

While many Christians believe there is a single ideal mate for each person to marry (if God intends them to ever marry), others believe that God gives more latitude and provides more possibilities.

Those singles in the first camp often get anxious wondering, "Is this *the* person for me?" Those in the latter category believe that since marriage is primarily a commitment of the will, there are probably a number of potential mates who meet the criteria of being a Christian, having similar values, etc. "You could serve God and be happy with any number of different potential mates," they are fond of saying.

We won't attempt to solve that great debate here. Let's just say that unless, like Isaac of the Old Testament, your parents have a servant they can send out on a mission to find you a prospective spouse, you're going to have to sort through the prospects yourself. How can you know if a person you are dating is the person you should consider meeting at the altar?

We already know that good looks aren't enough. Outer beauty (or handsomeness) is a pathetic foundation upon which to build a relationship. If that's all you've got, what are you going to do when the wrinkles come, the muscles sag, the pounds appear, and the hair falls out? If God doesn't judge by outer appearance, neither should we (1 Samuel 16:7). What's in the heart matters far more.

The prospect of financial security isn't sufficient. The nation's phone books are filled with names of miserable couples (many in the process of "uncoupling"). Money isn't the problem for many of these. They are on solid economic footing, but something else—far more important—is missing.

The biggest issue for Christians is whether the person in question shares your faith in Jesus Christ. If you are a believer, and she is not (or vice versa), it's a no-brainer. That's *not* the person for you. You don't even have to pray about it. God has already drawn a boundary that you'd be really wise NOT to cross (2 Corinthians 6:14–18).

More Great Quotes

"Keep your eyes wide open before marriage, half shut afterwards."
—Benjamin Franklin

WOW!

Ken Taylor's college experience of looking for the "perfect" girl, and an upperclassman's comment, "Look, if you *could* find a perfect girl, she wouldn't marry *you*"!

GOOD QUESTIONS TO ASK YOURSELF WHEN PONDERING A POTENTIAL MATE

1. Has this relationship enhanced or diminished my love for and commitment to Christ?
2. Do we share the same spiritual values and priorities?
3. Could I do more for Christ and His kingdom married to this person than not?
4. What do those older and wiser believers who know me best and love me most think about this relationship?
5. Do I *respect* this person? Or do I often feel embarrassed/ashamed of his/her actions?
6. Do I enjoy talking and just being with this person (without physical intimacy)?

7. If we took away our physical attraction/involvement, what substance would be left in this relationship?
8. Do we argue repeatedly and heatedly over lots of issues?
9. How much time and effort have I spent seeking God's will in this relationship?
10. How well do we *really* know one another? Have we seen each other in a wide variety of situations over an adequate period of time?

It is a wise course of action to also discuss these questions with a spiritual mentor (i.e., an older, wiser, godly person you know). This individual needs to be objective and willing to ask you hard, uncomfortable questions.

BEING HELD ACCOUNTABLE

WHAT IS ACCOUNTABILITY?

Accountability is that process wherein we "give an account." We report on a situation. Someone keeps tabs on us; they routinely ask us hard questions to make us analyze and evaluate what we are doing and why. Accountability provides an objective "check-up" on our actions and motives.

The result is that we are less driven by pure emotion (or hormones), and forced to think and reason with God's help. By constantly comparing our relationship to the standards of God's Word, we are less likely to get into trouble.

Who can hold you accountable?

CATCH A CLUE

- A parent or grandparent
- A leader in your church who's happily, healthily married
- An older, wiser Christian friend
- A pastor, youth pastor, college pastor
- A Bible study group
- A special accountability group (perhaps two or three other same-sex friends who are in dating relationships) where there is freedom to share openly and honestly

SAMPLE ACCOUNTABILITY QUESTIONS

1. How is God being honored in your relationship this week?

2. Is anything currently taking place in your relationship that is spiritually questionable? What?

3. Chart your relationship right now on the following scale.

I	2	3	4	5	6	7	8	9	10
Self-centeredness									God-centeredness

I	2	3	4	5	6	7	8	9	10
Poor (or little) communication									Great communication

I	2	3	4	5	6	7	8	9	10
Lots of unresolved conflict							Excellence in conflict resolution		

I	2	3	4	5	6	7	8	9	10
Sexual impurity									Sexual purity

I	2	3	4	5	6	7	8	9	10

Spiritual complacency/apathy   Spiritual health & vitality

I	2	3	4	5	6	7	8	9	10

An exclusive focus on "US"   A servanthood/outward focus

I	2	3	4	5	6	7	8	9	10

Unhealthy isolation   Rich involvement with others

I	2	3	4	5	6	7	8	9	10

Dysfunctional dependence   Healthy interdependence

I	2	3	4	5	6	7	8	9	10

Grimness/joylessness   Joy/fun/laughter

I	2	3	4	5	6	7	8	9	10

A bad example to the world   A good advertisement for Christ

What specifics caused you to grade your relationship as you did?
What do you need to do to raise your low marks on the chart above?

4. How can I/this group better pray for you and "spur [you] on toward love and good deeds" (Hebrews 10:24) in your dating relationship? Give me/us some specifics.

LISTENING TO PARENTS' INPUT

THEY BROUGHT YOU INTO THIS WORLD

They tried (in most cases) to do their best at the difficult, mysterious task of "parenting."

They failed. Often. Sometimes miserably. Sometimes *terribly*. The result is that you almost assuredly bear some emotional scars.

But look beyond all the mistakes, and remember a couple of things. First, every parent is, in the truest sense, an amateur, a raw rookie. The hospital doesn't give new moms and pops a comprehensive course in how to rear children before releasing them. Nope. They hand the terrified couple a squirming infant (and a HUGE bill!) and then they're on their own. It's up to them to learn "on the job," so to speak.

A second thing to remember is that (in all but the worst cases), parents deeply love their kids and want the best for them. We're betting your folks are no exception. They may not express their concerns very tactfully, or go about giving advice in the desired way, but a big part of what drives them is a desperate desire to protect you and keep you from making bad choices. They know first-hand the pain of foolish decisions. Most parents would give anything if they could keep their children from making the same mistakes they made.

So cut your folks some slack, and then take five really wise steps.

FIVE WISE STEPS

1. Ask your folks about their dating experiences.

Face it. They've been around the block a few times. They've probably encountered more than a few manipulators, users, and jerks. Find out what they did right, what they did wrong. Their stories are often surprising, even fascinating. Inquire what they would do differently if they had the chance to do "the dating thing" all over again.

2. Listen.

Yep, they're from a different generation, and times have changed. But true wisdom is timeless. Don't tune them out! You can learn something valuable—even from a Dad who is hopelessly old-fashioned, or a Mom whose last dating experience was 25 years ago. This is a big part of what it means to "honor your father and mother" (Ephesians 6:2).

3. Fight the tendency to be defensive.

Maybe it comes from having lived together for so long or from knowing each others' quirks too well, but something about parent-child relations often means fireworks. Why is it that we angrily reject the advice of a parent, only to turn around and accept the exact same counsel from a friend? Practice focusing more on WHAT your parents are saying, than on HOW they are saying it.

4. Share your dating dilemmas.

The very notion of this is shocking to some, but many young adults are pleasantly surprised when they involve their parents in the dating equation. Older folks often have an uncanny sense of discernment. They can smell a rat. They can see trouble ahead. They can provide encouragement to keep doing right. If you exclude them from this part of your life, you are overlooking a treasure chest of wisdom.

5. When appropriate, put their wisdom to work.

It takes humility for us to admit our parents are right. But often they are. And remember, of all the people in the world, they probably know us best, and love us most. Doesn't it make sense to at least consider following advice from such a source?

DON'T FORGET

The Bad News

"No matter how old you get, in your parents' minds, you will always have the wisdom and emotional maturity of Beaver Cleaver."—Dave Barry

WHAT'S THE BOTTOM LINE?

Parents can be an invaluable resource in helping you determine, "is this the one?" Unfortunately many young adults ignore the potential help that is so near by.

Our counsel is for you to get input from your parents. What have you got to lose?

SECTION 10
SEX AND PURITY

SEX: SHOULD WE OR SHOULDN'T WE?

SEX

Titillating billboards, sensual magazine covers, explicit scenes in mainstream movies, erotic song lyrics—the fact is our culture is in hormonal overdrive. Yeah, yeah, illicit sex has *always* been a part of the human drama, but no era has ever been so sexually charged as ours.

A generation or so ago, author C. S. Lewis wondered about our obsession with sex in his classic book *Mere Christianity*. Citing the popularity of strip clubs, he posed an interesting question: What if instead of watching girls undress publicly, crowds gathered in theaters to watch someone lift the cover off a plate of food, revealing, ever so briefly, a lamb chop. "Would you not think that in that country something had gone wrong with the appetite for food?"

It's a good question, and a fair one. Something has clearly gone awry. Maybe we've forgotten the purpose of sex?

WHY DID GOD INVENT SEX?

Huge tomes have been written about the essence of sex. Even theologians have weighed in with their lengthy opinions. But when you boil it all down, the Bible seems to state two broad reasons or purposes for sex.

1. *To propagate*. At the most obvious level, sex serves the important function of perpetuating our species. "Be fruitful and increase in number and fill the

earth," God told Noah and his sons (Genesis 9:1). Clearly one of the most enjoyable commands God ever gave His creatures! The point? It's like the profound old saying, "If your parents never, ever had sex, chances are you won't either." No sex = No human race!

2. *To celebrate*. Within the lifelong covenant of marriage, sex was designed by God to model on a physical level, a couple's spiritual and emotional intimacy, love, and commitment. Contrary to popular opinion, the Biblical view of sex is *not* prudish. The Old Testament book Song of Songs is a fairly explicit celebration of physical love between a husband and wife. From the sound of it, this was a couple who had quite a honeymoon!

What conclusion can we draw? Sex is wonderful and good and to be thoroughly enjoyed in its rightful place. When we follow the designer's guidelines, there is the potential to have a wildly fulfilling sex life!

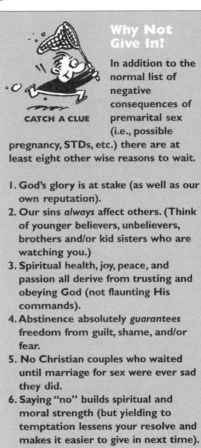

CATCH A CLUE

Why Not Give In?

In addition to the normal list of negative consequences of premarital sex (i.e., possible pregnancy, STDs, etc.) there are at least eight other wise reasons to wait.

1. God's glory is at stake (as well as our own reputation).
2. Our sins *always* affect others. (Think of younger believers, unbelievers, brothers and/or kid sisters who are watching you.)
3. Spiritual health, joy, peace, and passion all derive from trusting and obeying God (not flaunting His commands).
4. Abstinence absolutely *guarantees* freedom from guilt, shame, and/or fear.
5. No Christian couples who waited until marriage for sex were ever sad they did.
6. Saying "no" builds spiritual and moral strength (but yielding to temptation lessens your resolve and makes it easier to give in next time).
7. The devil is an expert at using sexual failure to derail Christians.
8. Break ups are far less emotionally devastating when there's been no sexual involvement.

WHY SEX IS SUCH AN ISSUE

Like every good gift of God, sex can be misused. The goal of our enemy Satan is simple: to ruin our lives, if not outright destroy us (John 10:10; 1 Peter 5:8). His plan is first to tempt us to doubt the goodness of God and the plan of God (Genesis 3). If he succeeds here, he is then in perfect position to deceive and blind people (John 8:44; 2 Corinthians 4:4) to the truth.

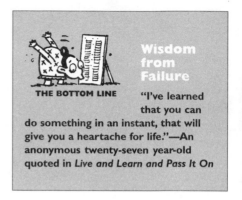

Wisdom from Failure

THE BOTTOM LINE "I've learned that you can do something in an instant, that will give you a heartache for life."—An anonymous twenty-seven year-old quoted in *Live and Learn and Pass It On*

It's a thoroughly devilish process. He appeals to our normal physical desires that have been distorted by sin. He uses the world (i.e., culture, society) to paint an appealing (but very twisted) view of sex. He capitalizes on our love of pleasure, our desire for immediate gratification, our tendency to not think about long-term consequences, and our common failure to keep our physical desires in check through a disciplined lifestyle.

The result is an immensely powerful urge that cuts to the core of who we are as sexual creatures. Succumbing to such temptations is like caving in to the alluring promises of narcotics. Sex degenerates into nothing more than a short-term shot of physical pleasure, a way of momentarily numbing one's self to the pains and worries of real life. It can become all-consuming, and when it does, like all addictions, it carries a *huge* price tag.

BEFORE YOUR DATE

A lot of couples are *reactive*. That is, they don't have any clear goals or direction. They passively wait for circumstances to arise and then they react. With this kind of weak resolve they often end up in sexual trouble. By not putting any safeguards in place, by not having firmly established bound- aries beforehand, they allowed events (perhaps *hormones* is the better word?) to dictate their destiny.

DON'T FORGET

Too Late

Once you're up to your neck in alligators, it's too late to talk about draining the swamp.

Far better to be *proactive*. What does that mean? Proactive couples think ahead. They know it's almost impossible to make wise decisions when they are setting Guinness' World Records on the sexual arousal scale. So they establish firm, clear boundaries beforehand. They plan (and pray) accordingly.

WHAT DO YOU WANT?

In his book *The Seven Habits of Highly Effective People,* Stephen Covey talks about how important it is to "begin with the end in mind." Essentially this is nothing more than peeking into the future, deciding what you want to end up with, and then figuring out what it will take to get there. If you bring this principle over into the realm of sex and dating, it can become a valuable tool for helping you set sexual standards.

Do you want guilt, shame, emotional stress, a relationship based on physical pleasure, a likely nasty break up, regret, an unplanned pregnancy, a distant and unsatisfying relationship with God, damage to your reputation (and God's!)? If that's the end you have in mind, then go for it. Have all the premarital sex you can!

But if you'd rather end up with a clear conscience, no fear, no regrets, a good reputation, a strong witness, moral purity and strength, a satisfying sense of being self-controlled (rather than at the mercy of your lust), then you need to set some boundaries that will help you resist sexual urges until marriage.

Some Boundaries to Consider

Every couple is different. What may prove especially enticing for one, may *not* be tempting for another. But here are some general guidelines that have helped a number of couples (or, in some cases, that *would have helped* had they been set and followed.)

CATCH A CLUE

- No watching sexually explicit movies. (You don't need any more ideas!)
- No conversations about sexual issues. (This is really unnecessary ... and dangerous!)
- No lingering around after the plans for the evening are concluded. (Make a plan, do the plan, then *go home!*)
- No changing into "something more comfortable." (This is nothing more than pushing over the first domino.)
- No getting alone in a bedroom. (Duh! Remember: The bedroom is for *sleeping*.)
- No turning out the lights. (The first recorded words of God in the Bible? "Let there be light.")
- No getting horizontal. (A hundred things can happen when you lie down; all of them are bad!)
- No touching of buttons or zippers (by either party!).
- No removal of any clothing. (If anything, keep *adding* clothing throughout your evening! By the end of the date, you each want to look like the Michelin man.)
- No extended kissing sessions. (In the arousal process, God designed kisses to lead to bigger and better things. Why get worked up for something you can't have right now?)

STRIVING FOR PURITY

DON'T GIVE IN

Some years ago, actors Micheal Keaton and Terri Garr starred in a movie called *Mr. Mom*. The plot went like this: *He* gets laid off. *She* goes back to work. *He* becomes a stay-at-home dad. Family unravels. Marital fireworks begin. At the end of the film a very attractive neighbor comes on to Keaton's character in an all-out seduction. Although he is sorely tempted (and feels he *might* even be able to get away with this infidelity), his conclusion is simple: I'm not going to give in to this, because the truest thing about me is that I'm in love with my wife.

Perhaps there's no better picture of how to remain pure than that.

Let's say, for the sake of argument, you've met "the one" (we can dream, can't we?). Now, the sexual heat is on. The temptations to express your love physically are fierce and unrelenting. Most nights your hormones could care less about potential consequences. "NOW!" they scream.

Given all this, is there any way to maintain personal purity? Absolutely. You can do the following four things.

1. Look back.

By "look back", we mean take some time to mentally rehearse where you've been. Look back on prior relationships. Were they pure? If so, imagine how bad you'd feel now if they had not been. If you were sexually active, recall briefly all the pain your impurity caused. Don't wallow in it, but let those unpleasant memories serve as a warning buzzer to you now.

By "look back", we also mean to look back to the time when you put your faith in Christ. *You* made a commitment. *He* made you a brand new person inside (2 Corinthians 5:17). Sure, you still have sexual urges, but now at the deepest level of your soul your desire is to please God. How could it be otherwise? You have the actual Holy Spirit of God living inside you (1Corinthians 6:19)! He has made it so that you now "participate in the divine nature" (2 Peter 1:4). In short, there is something of God alive in you that *always* wants to do the right thing. You may not FEEL all this, but if the Gospel is true, these are the facts. You have a new nature that can (and should) be cultivated and fed.

2. Look around.

By "look around," we mean note the couples around you. Consider the ones who are sexually active. Look at the problems they're encountering because of their misuse of God's good gift of sex. Also study the couples who are dating "by the book" (i.e., according to the principles of God's Word). All around you are examples, both good and bad. Watch them all and learn from them all.

You're young...so what?

THE BIBLE SAYS

"Don't let anyone look down on you because you are young, but set an example for the believers in ... purity." (I Timothy 4:12)

3. Look ahead.

By "look ahead," we mean glimpse into the future at what you'd eventually like to have in terms of a relationship. Do you want an unplanned pregnancy? Do you want to one day be forced to have a conversation with your spouse (or child) about how promiscuous you were prior to marriage? Do you want to experience that awful sense of being alienated from God because you've chosen to reject His plan for your life?

Dumb questions, right? *Nobody* wants those things. *Nobody* ever sets out to "achieve" such things. And yet, lots of people experience those heartaches, simply because they didn't think ahead. Don't make that same mistake.

[For more on this topic, see the previous chapter on "Setting Standards Before Your Date."]

4. Look up.

This may be the most important of the four steps. By "look up," we mean call on God for divine help. Left to ourselves we are weak and pitiful creatures. However, when we link our puny faith with the infinite resources of God, we find an other-worldly strength.

This is not a suggestion that you call to God only when you're in the throes of sexual temptation. It's a plea that you build a strong and vital, moment-by-moment relationship with Jesus Christ. Apart from that, you probably don't stand a chance.

The conclusion? The best way to say "No!" to sin (especially powerful sexual temptations) is to say a prior and a bigger and a continual "YES!" to God.

PRACTICING SELF-CONTROL

KEEP OR LOSE CONTROL

A few years ago The Pointer Sisters sang that immortal song that defined the sexual yearnings of youth—"I'm riding down the freeway of love in my pink Cadillac."

Okay, on second thought, that was Aretha Franklin. The Pointers' big hit went something like this—"I'm so excited, and I just can't hide it. I'm about to lose control and I think I like it." Can you think of any other song that so masterfully portrays the power of sexual attraction?

Okay, almost every song on the radio since Marconi invented the wireless. But you get the point. Sexual self-control is a difficult proposition. Especially for Christians living in a generation that says, "If it feels good, do it." Remember, it's our era that has deemed W-A-I-T to be the ultimate in four-letter words.

Meanwhile, back in the Bible, here's the word from on high:

- Proverbs 25:28, "Like a city whose walls are broken down is a man who lacks self-control."
- Galatians 5:22-23, "But the fruit of the Spirit is … self-control."
- 2 Timothy 3:1-3, "But mark this: There will be terrible times in the last days. People will be … without self-control."

So how do we do it? What's the secret to practicing self-control?

KEEPING CONTROL

Here are some better ways to fight the self-control battle. They aren't foolproof, but they're better than plunging repeatedly into a mountain pool.

ABC'S OF SELF-CONTROL

Acknowledge your weakness.
Until we admit we have problems in this area, we'll never really turn fully to God to find help and hope.

Be filled with God's Spirit.
Galatians 5 tells us that self-control is really an issue of being controlled or empowered by the Holy Spirit. Ask God to fill you with His Spirit (Ephesians 5:18) so that you can live as you should.

Commit to an accountability relationship.
God has designed us in such a way that we need other people. We need their encouragement, prayers, even their rebukes and correction. A friend or small group with whom you can be gut-level honest is a wonderful resource in the battle for self-control.

WOW!

Advice from Previous Generations for Dealing with Moments of Strong Sexual Temptation

- Jump in a frigid mountain pool/take a cold shower
- Go to the convent/monastery to live
- Run around the block a few times
- Read the Bible/memorize Scripture
- Pray
- Go bale some hay/lift weights
- Wear a chastity belt
- Gnaw the leg off a coffee table
- Do some homework (especially algebra problems)
- Sing hymns
- Think about starving children around the world

DIFFERENCES BETWEEN MEN AND WOMEN

A REAL DIFFERENCE

Besides the obvious anatomical differences, and the fact that NASA researchers now believe males are from the planet Mars and females originated on Venus (a fact all but confirmed by several best selling "non-fiction" books), the sexes are quite unique.

Consider that these are *broad* generalizations with *a large number of* exceptions, but still accurate in many instances:

Men tend to be ...	*Women tend to be ...*
More physical	More verbal
Physically stronger	Physically weaker
Compartmental in their thinking	"Global"/holistic in their thinking
Oblivious to feelings	More in touch with feelings
Goal-oriented	People/need-oriented
Logical thinkers	Intuitive thinkers
Eager to achieve	Eager to belong
More assured	More in need of assurance
Dependent on work for significance	Dependent on husband and family for significance
Wired to watch 47 channels at once	Wired to watch one program at a time
Too proud to ask for help	Too smart NOT to ask for help

Men tend to be ... (continued)	**Women tend to be...(continued)**
Into movies like *Dumb & Dumber*	Into movies like *Jane Eyre* & *Howard's End*
More aware of the *models* in the *Sports Illustrated* swimsuit issue	More drawn to the actual *swimsuits*
Sexually aroused by sight	Sexually aroused by touch

DEALING WITH THE DIFFERENCES

Okay, all this talk about the sexes. Now what? Well, we have several options. We can:

    a. **Deny** *the differences.* This makes about as much sense as denying the Law of Gravity. Men and women are fundamentally different and all the social engineering in the world can't alter this truth! Neither sex is better; each is distinct and unique.

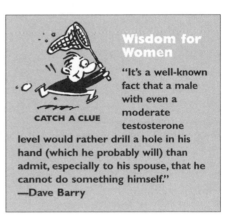

CATCH A CLUE

Wisdom for Women

"It's a well-known fact that a male with even a moderate testosterone level would rather drill a hole in his hand (which he probably will) than admit, especially to his spouse, that he cannot do something himself."
—Dave Barry

    b. **Ignore** *the differences.* Why not take advantage of life-enhancing, relationship-enriching information?

    c. **Seek to understand** *the differences.* A wise man or woman will make his or her sweetheart/spouse a subject of long-term, intense scrutiny. You will never figure him/her out. The human soul has depths no one but God knows. But you can, with effort, learn to move on to the next phase.

d. **Accept** *the differences.* Imagine how dull the world would be if we didn't have the opposite sex around to shake our heads at. Sure, they're weird, but in a fascinating kind of way.

e. **Celebrate** *the differences.* Don't just tolerate the opposite sex! Celebrate God's genius! In perfect wisdom He made it so that when Adam and Eve came together like a two-piece jigsaw puzzle, they formed a new entity, something whole and complete. (And note that He pronounced it "very good"!) Nothing has changed through the ages. There's still a wonderfully satisfying fit when a husband and wife bring their wildly different personalities, perspectives, attitudes, and bodies together and connect spiritually, emotionally, and physically.

Wisdom for Men

Young son: Is what I heard true, Dad, that in some parts of Africa a man doesn't **wow!** know his wife until he marries her?

Dad: That happens in every country, son.

It's a miracle that such diverse creatures could ever be called "one." But that's precisely what God does!

SECTION 11

DATE IDEAS

CREATIVE DATING

HERE ARE 52 DATE IDEAS

- No talking allowed for the whole evening. You must use gestures and/or facial expressions to communicate.
- Visit a nursing home and talk with some of the residents about what dating was like in their teenage years.
- Find some great-looking/sounding recipes in magazines like *Better Homes & Gardens* or *Southern Living*. Go to the grocery store, buy the necessary ingredients, and come home and cook a gourmet meal.
- Dress up in clown outfits and make-up and visit children in the local hospital.
- Volunteer to baby-sit for someone (this is often a great way to remind hormone-crazed couples to cool it … or else!)
- At the library, check out some joke/riddle books and take turns telling each other jokes.
- Visit a cemetery and read grave markers. Speculate about the lives and deaths of the "residents."
- Take an underprivileged kid to the park or to a big toy store for a few hours.
- Take a bike hike to a nearby community and look for something or someone interesting and unusual.
- Draw portraits of each other. Take up to an hour a piece, and then compare the results. Warning: No throwing sketch pads at each other.
- Go to a play at a nearby college or high school. Live drama is usually much more entertaining than movies (or dead drama).

- Celebrate offbeat holidays like Groundhog Day or National Vienna Sausage Week. Throw a party and invite your friends.
- Have a theme date. For example: France. Eat french fries with French's® mustard and chase it down with french vanilla ice cream. Speak French to each other, and watch a video documentary about France (usually available for check-out at the library).
- Go to a mall and walk around speaking a made-up language to each other. Watch the reactions of people.
- Build your own volcano (with sand, dirt, baking soda and vinegar).
- Watch one of the many "religious" films made by Hollywood over the years (e.g. *Jesus of Nazareth*, *The Ten Commandments*), and compare it to what the Bible really says.
- Have a decathlon competition with the following ten events:
  - Have a paper airplane throw (longest-lasting flight)
  - Have a shoe-kick (hang shoe off the end of your toes and then fling it forward for distance)
  - Have a book-balancing (on your head for the longest time)
  - Have a staring contest (without blinking)
  - Hold that note (see who can sing/hum a note the longest without taking a breath)
  - Have a lemon suck (who can do it without making a face)
  - Have a water gulp (who can drink a big, full glass first)
  - Do a seed spit (who can spit a watermelon, apple, or orange seed the farthest)
  - Have an ambidextrous test (who can write the alphabet with their "weak" hand most neatly and legibly—get someone else to judge)
  - Throw cards in the hat (who can flip the most cards—out of 52—into a hat from a distance of six feet)
- Watch *Jeopardy* together and actually keep track of points.
- Buy cheap squirt guns and go for it.
- Have a sock bomb fight. Get about 20 pairs of balled up socks, sit on the

floor about 12 feet apart, and have it out. (NOTE: The socks don't hurt when they hit you, and this is a great way to get your aggression out!)

- Take turns reading your favorite short stories and/or poems to each other.
- Invent your own comic strip (characters, story line, artistic style, etc.).
- Buy some kind of strange meat at the grocery/butcher shop: shark, buffalo, squid, ostrich, etc., and experiment with different ways to cook it. Invent several different recipes. Have a taste test.
- Get an old beat-up piece of furniture for cheap. Strip it and refinish it.
- Get up early on a Saturday morning and go garage saling. Some of the greatest bargains in the world on all kinds of cool stuff can be found if you're willing to set your alarm clock early and do a little hunting.
- Play croquet (actually read the rules, set up the course, and have a serious contest).
- Buy matching yo-yos and spend the evening learning how to do some tricks.
- Get a friend to chauffeur you all over town; get another couple to cook a big meal for you. (You do it for them the following weekend.)
- Go to some restaurant you've never been to (and most likely wouldn't try). Large cities offer all kinds of culinary choices—Thai food, Ethiopian, soul food, Lebanese, etc. Sample some new cuisine.
- Take a sky-diving class together and then take the plunge.
- Go to the airport and watch the planes come and go. Daydream together about great cities you'd like to visit and why. There's great "people watching" at the airport!
- Go to a home improvement store (e.g. Lowe's, Home Depot, etc.) and watch one of the free demonstrations. Browse and point out to each other your favorite carpets, tiles, cabinets, etc.
- Try to see who can make each other laugh first.
- Put Walkman® headphones on and sing along to a tape. It's kind of like karaoke, except the person listening can only hear the singer's voice (and

it's usually off-key and hilarious). This is worth hours of fun, especially in a group dating situation.

- Go to a poetry reading at a local bookstore. This is quite an experience, sometimes bizarre, and often unintentionally funny. Also, you can sometimes meet famous authors if the store is sponsoring a book-signing.
- With two or three other couples, videotape your own "variety/comedy show." Then make some popcorn and watch it. Groan a lot.
- Get some bread and go feed the ducks at a pond in a nearby park. This is almost always a relaxing time and makes for good conversation.
- Take a Saturday morning and go on a silent retreat together. After separately spending time alone with God for, say, three hours, come back together for lunch and discuss what you learned or discovered.
- Go to the beach or to a big sandbox and make a giant sandcastle. Believe it or not, you'll learn a lot about each other working together on such a project.
- Take a class together (check with your local college, parks and recreation department, or vo-tech school)—juggling, ballroom dancing, basic auto repair.
- Make a date to go to a late-night coffeeshop, each with a scratch pad of paper, and work on your individual "life mission statements." This is an exercise in which you spell out what you hope to accomplish in life, what you feel your purpose in life should be. The end result is a document that can give you real direction and focus in life.
- Write a movie screenplay or a novel together. You may be the next Steven Spielberg or Jane Austen.
- Go to a discount store with $10 each, and put together a "care package" for a missionary family or friend in the military. Buy small, inexpensive, fun items that will surprise this person or family. Add some personal notes. Mail it to him/her/them.
- Get together with some other couples, make some sandwhiches, buy some

fruit and soft drinks, and distribute these to homeless people in a nearby urban area. Only do this in a group.

- Build a small campfire, and roast weenies and marshmallows.
- Borrow a telescope and go out into the country where it's really dark and do some stargazing. Watch for shooting stars. Look for E.T.
- Buy a couple of Slinkys® (very inexpensive) and spend the evening playing with them.
- Make chocolate chip cookies together and then feast on them, fresh out of the oven, with big glasses of cold milk.
- Plant a small vegetable garden together. See how much produce you can grow. This is good for LOTS of dates.
- Get a camera each and spend an evening seeing who can take the coolest photograph. Take the film to a one-hour developing place and compare the results.
- Invite another couple over and play a board game like Monopoly. Play in teams and establish a prize for the winning couple.
- Borrow a B.B. gun or sling shot, and go someplace safe for a little target practice, and shooting contest.

CHEAP DATES

HOW TO SAVE MONEY

- "Check out" the library. This is often the best kept secret in town: books, magazines, sometimes even video check-outs (for free!). Certain libraries also maintain special collections, for example a genealogy research room where you can trace your roots. Go hang out, especially on a rainy day.

- "Take a whiff" night. Drive around and try to see how many distinct odors you can identify. See who has the best olfactory glands.

CATCH A CLUE

Keep This in Mind

"Entertainment is expensive; fun is cheap."
—Steve Lawhead

- Visit a museum. If you live in or near a big city, this can be a cultural feast. If you live in a small town, you may have to settle for some offbeat attraction like the Dental Floss Hall of Fame or Bud's Gallery of Pine Cones. Either way, it's usually cheap and definitely different.

- Borrow a puppy or kitten for the evening, and laugh at its antics.

- Do some "people watching" at the mall. This may be the best entertainment in all the world! Humans are nothing if not quirky and fascinating. Look for people who resemble famous celebrities. Study people and try to guess what their background/story is.

- Browse in an antique store. It sounds like something only your Aunt Gertrude would want to do, but there's actually some pretty cool stuff in some of these funky old shops. It's like exploring a gigantic attic!
- Go watch Little League ball games. Unlike the pampered pros (many of whom are head cases and prima donnas), these little tikes play for the sheer joy of it. You'll laugh your head off, and watching the parents is an eye-opening experience.
- Explore a nearby warehouse discount store (e.g. Sam's) around noon or 5 in the evening, and sample all the free food they give out to try to entice buyers.
- Surf the Net together. You have to watch out for the trash, of course. But there's lots of interesting and off-the-wall stuff out there in Cyberspace. If you already have access, this won't cost you a penny.
- Do a random act of kindness for somebody. Rake an elderly neighbor's lawn. Run some errands for a harried housewife on your street. Provide two hours of free baby-sitting for that young couple who needs to get out. Donate some old clothes to the Salvation Army or Goodwill.
- Do something constructive together. Wash and vacuum your car(s). Do homework. Work on some creative Christmas gifts so that you're ready when the holidays arrive.
- Exercise. Take a walk (and have a talk). Play tennis at a public playground. Throw a Frisbee®. Go jogging or bike-riding. Go swimming. Rollerblade®. Hit a bucket of golf balls at the driving range.
- Do a project together. Clean out your closets. Have a garage sale with another couple or other friends.
- Buy one of those "Special Saver" coupon books from a group that is doing fund-raising. Though the initial cost might be $30-35, you'll have all kinds of great discounts and two-for-one offers, and the coupons are generally good for a whole year.

GREAT "GET TO KNOW YOU" DATES

THE PLACE TO START

What's the point of dating, if not to get to know a person better? How can you do that? Lots of ways!

- Look at old pictures/scrapbooks. A trip "down memory lane" can give you great insight into a person's background, into why they are the way they are. If he was raised by a family of wolves in Siberia, you need to know that little biographical tidbit!

- Play the "Sixty Minutes" game. That's where you take turns interviewing each other for thirty minutes apiece. Ask all kinds of questions about the past, present, and future. Inquire about values, opinions on current events, interests, hobbies, and beliefs. The only two rules are: (1) You DON'T have to answer any question that makes you feel uncomfortable; and, (2) If you DO answer, you must be honest.

- Do a jigsaw puzzle. Yep, we know. It sounds about as exciting as reading the phone book together; however, there's something about this quiet activity that generates really good conversation. The upside? You get to work together on a goal, and it takes a long time. The downside? He/she might be the sort who hides the last piece in order to be able to say, "Nyah, nyah, nyah, nyah, nyah! *I* finished the puzzle!"

- Life stories. Take turns sharing about your life—big events, influential people, major accomplishments, profound disappointments. You can either proceed *chronologically* ("I was born in a cab in Peoria, and then …") or *topically* ("Educationally, I … occupationally, I … spiritually, I …")

- Take a day hike. Go to a park or wilderness area. You'll have ample time to converse on the way there, and being in the great outdoors with a goal (e.g. "we're going to hike down into that canyon and then back") will give you a shared sense of purpose. You'll be partners in a common task.

- Do a service project. On your basic Friday or Saturday night date, it's common to try to: look your best, be on your best behavior, put your best foot forward—in short to come across as better than you really are! On the other hand, doing a service project together (i.e. helping someone in need) gets the focus off yourselves, and brings out what's really inside your hearts. There's no quicker way to find out whether a person is giving, hard-working, compassionate, selfless, and/or impatient.

- Attempt something neither of you knows how to do. Go play golf, or try your hand at roller blading, or attempting to change the oil in your cars. Venturing into "uncharted waters" takes real guts and a good sense of humor, but it reveals volumes about a person. How does he react to failure? Can she poke fun at herself? Before you get serious with a person, wouldn't you like to know if he has a temper, or if she's got a problem with pride?

PLACES YOU WON'T GET TO KNOW EACH OTHER

If the goal of dating is to get to know one another in a way that honors God and encourages the other person, then we can rule out a number of options and places for a date.

1. The Movies
BORING! LAME! BAD CHOICE!
Think about it. You sit next to each other, staring straight ahead, not talking (unless you're one of those rude movie patrons) for two solid hours! You

could do *that* separately, at home, and for a lot less money. This is not to say couples should NEVER go to the movies or watch a video together. But early on in a relationship, this is a terrible, lazy, foolish, dumb way to try to get to know someone. (By the way, did we mention this is *not* a good way to get to know each other?)

2. A Rock Concert

Let's analyze this option.
You stand (usually) in a sea of humanity; get pushed and poked, maybe even picked up against your will and "surfed" across the auditorium or stadium; you expose your ears to deafening (literally!) noise (only the Space Shuttle is louder); you endure monumental traffic jams before and after the event; and you spend a truckload of cash doing it.

When it's all said and done, you have a good story or two ("Hey, how 'bout that guy who heaved all over your purse! Heh. Heh."), but you really haven't had much of a chance to interact. Save this kind of activity for down the road.

3. A Football/Basketball/Baseball Game

Let's face it. This is simply a combination of numbers 1 and 2 above. It's a very loud spectator sport (unless we're talking about golf, where talking is strictly forbidden, and where the chances are you'll both fall asleep, thus opening yourselves up to the accusation of "having slept together!"), at which many men forget they're even with a female. The typical male ends up watching intently, cheering, doing the wave, high-fiving total strangers, sneaking peeks at the scantily clad cheerleaders, and screaming at the officials. If there's to be any conversation, it can only be during time-outs, or between innings, and then, he wants to talk about blitzes, dunks, and suicide squeeze plays, *not* his feelings about the relationship.

Even when the game is over, it's not over. If his team *wins*, he'll treat you to an interminable verbal replay of the whole event (never mind the fact that you WERE actually there). On the other hand, if his team *loses*, the trip home will conist of a litany of all the dumb decisions the coach made, and the bonehead plays of the members of the special team.

In one sense, athletic contests *are* a good opportunity for women to at least observe men in their genuine, "unguarded" glory. But alas, women, *don't* go to a sporting event expecting much in the way of relational interaction.

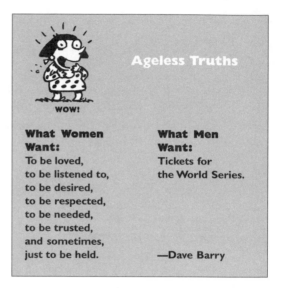

Ageless Truths

WOW!

What Women Want:
To be loved, to be listened to, to be desired, to be respected, to be needed, to be trusted, and sometimes, just to be held.

What Men Want:
Tickets for the World Series.

—Dave Barry

4. *Your Bedroom*

A lot of things can happen to a dating couple in a bedroom, and most of them are not good (oh, they're *fun* and *physically pleasurable,* but they do *not* make for a healthy dating relationship).

The goal of dating is to get to know one another emotionally, spiritually, and socially, not physically. (That's a bonus for married couples only, and for good reason. See the "Sex and Purity" section.)

SECTION 12
GROUP DATING

WHAT'S A GROUP DATE?

GIVE IT A TRY

For those who tire of traditional forms of social engagement for a variety of reasons may want to try Group Dating as a positive alternative. Instead of tables for two, group dates are filling college campuses and coffeehouses as a not-so new but definitely refreshing counter-culture.

In a group date, guys and girls from work, class or your neighborhood get together for an endless variety of group-structured activities. Softball games, drive-in movies, water-skiing at the lake are some of the more popular settings for helping people develop friendships without the pretense of date-dating. Some people within the group may go on to develop personal relationships as a result, but group dating is not to be confused with a marketplace mentality. When it's done right, it is fueled by pure motives with no hidden agendas. People are simply discovering that the best relationships are not necessarily exclusive ones. And a foundation of friendship is hard to beat when it comes to making relationships that last.

THE ESSENTIALS FOR A GROUP DATE:

No coupling off...even just "to talk." Save it for later on the phone if you need to.

No pressure...nothing that absolutely requires an opposite-sex partner or pairing off. Some things like dancing, games, etc. take a new twist just by switching partners throughout the evening!

No expectations…everyone knows they'll pay their own way. This avoids awkwardness or feelings of obligation.

Whatever you do, be willing to have fun. Where a twosome might lack the spontaneity and freedom to enjoy these suggestions (or even be a nightmare!), these can be a blast with the right group and the right attitude.

NEW ATTITUDE

Group dating is a new attitude toward what relationships are all about. It puts the age-old question to the test: "Can a man and a woman just be friends?" Those who have tried group dating may have a surprising answer for the Harrys and Sallys who are wondering the same thing! Group dating challenges traditional definitions of the purpose of dating (a means to an end) by giving pure friendship a shot.

CATCH A CLUE

Group Date Testimonies

"One year in college, we hosted a dinner party for our group of guy and girl friends. We spent the day shopping together for all the special ingredients. We cooked together—some in the kitchen, some setting the table up with "real" plates we borrowed from the campus dining hall! We made it like an Italian bistro and served each other like real waiters with towels over our arms! Everyone had a great time and a great meal!"— Kirsten, Witchita, KS

"One night after work, my buddies and I called each other up and decided to meet at our old high school football stadium. We backed up a guy's truck to the fence and played our favorite music while we started a major ultimate frisbee game! The setting was great as it brought back lots of funny memories from our high school days. And everyone got the stress-of-the-day out on the field! Afterwards, we cooled off with sodas from a local diner."—Alan, Grand Rapids, MI

WHAT'S SO GOOD ABOUT GROUP DATING?
BEYOND HORMONES

Group dating is showing up as a valid recommendation from relationship experts all over the place. Studies show that friendship is the most important factor in a long-lasting romantic relationship. Anyone with hormones can be a great "couple," but for two people to make it for the long-haul, the foundation of friendship has to be there.

CATCH A CLUE

Date a Friend, not a Stranger

"My best dates were with friends—guys I already knew. My worst dates were with strangers— set-ups I barely knew at all."
—**Susan, Houston, Texas**

In a group setting, you get to observe a potential dating partner in a real context. It's too easy to put your foot in your mouth rather than your best foot forward when you are trying to impress someone on an exclusive date. In a more relaxed setting, everyone is more comfortable being themselves. Watching how a person handles their temper in a softball game or how they interact with your own friends tells you a lot about that person you might not observe on a first date.

Discernment is a valuable tool when it comes to dating. Finding out the most information you can about a person before investing in a personal relationship can help you to make better dating decisions.

FROM GROUP TO EXCLUSIVE

FAVORED ATTRACTION

If you happen to find yourself particularly attracted to one member of a group of friends, that's great! It doesn't mean you have to ditch the group-thing. Nor does it mean you have to ignore your feelings for the sake of the group. When it's done right, group dating serves a great purpose of providing an environment where real love can grow.

Here are some hints for those in the "initial" stage of growing attraction between two people within a group setting. Follow the acrostic "S-L-O" for a reminder to pace the relationship:

CATCH A CLUE

Us & Them

A group of us met up for dinner every Thursday after work. When I saw David, one of my guy friends' new buddies, I hoped to get to know him better. Turns out, I didn't even end up sitting by him during dinner! But I watched him laugh at the table and really paid attention to the way he seemed to listen when others talked to him. Well, over the next few weeks, we did end up side by side at dinner more than once. And when he finally asked me out, we made a date to work out at the gym before we met "the gang" for dinner. Now, several gym-and-dinner dates later, we still hang out with our friends. Balancing our "couple time" with hanging with the gang has kept us from excluding ourselves while we have grown closer together."
—**April, Traverse City, Michigan**

S—*Slow down*. Take it slow before you try solo! Group dating is not like shopping for jeans—trying on every pair on until one "fits" just right. In some groups, no one ever ends up dating. And that's fine!

L—*Look*...before you leap. You may feel adrenaline coursing through your veins the very first time you see the "new girl" in the group. But get to know her in this setting well, so when you do go out, you'll be on a date with a friend you know well.

O—*One-on-One Time*. If the gang is getting together for a late show Saturday evening, plan to grab an early dinner together as some one-on-one time for the two of you. Then meet up with everyone else for the show. In other words, do something that doesn't take up the whole evening, so you can still attach some group time to your night together.

THINGS THAT MAKE A GROUP GAG!

(Or Guidelines for Dating within a Group)

P.D.A.

Remember the summer church camp rule: No PDA (Public Display of Affection)? Well, maybe those conservative counselors knew what they were talking about! Everyone knows what it's like to be around a couple engrossed in each other—and it can be pretty obnoxious. The hand slid comfortably into the backpocket. The "stolen" kiss that smacks loud enough for everyone nearby to hear. The giggles. The secrets whispered back and forth.

If you have any respect for your friends (and want to be respected), think back to those summer days and keep the PDA rule. "Consideration" is the language spoken here. No one will question your masculinity if you keep your hands to yourself. Holding hands, a peck on the cheek, no problem. But spare the groping, please. Maturity might make a better impression on your friends when they see your restraint. Just be considerate of others when you're in the group—being buddies in mixed company and a couple on your own time will go a long way.

BREAK UPS

Nothing is worse for group camaraderie than a break up between mutual friends. Soon alliances are made between his friends and hers and "he said"/ "she said" snowballs into a huge rift. Any relationship is bound to encounter trouble at one time or another. Unfortunately, when a romantic relationship blossoms from friendship among a group, the matter is hardly private. If you're considering dating a person in your "gang" of friends, think about the consequences on the group if things don't work out. Will you have the maturity to remain friends?

BONUS FOR "BREAK UPS"

By the way, if you're not part of the relationship between two people, remember: You're not part of the relationship! If a couple in your group is going through some problems, resist the temptation to make updates on the status of their relationship a mainstay of group conversation. Christians are particularly vulnerable to making other people's problems public disguised as a "prayer request." If you're concerned about a couple, pray for them. But don't discuss their problems simply because it's among friends.

SECTION 13

DATING GAMES PEOPLE PLAY (BUT THEY SHOULDN'T)

FLIRTING AND SIGNALS

THE BIG GAME

Dating is, in many ways, like a big "game." That means it has complicated rules and lots of built-in unpredictability. As with any game, some are more experienced or more adept. And that means—here's the bad news—at the end of every dating day, you'll find "winners and losers."

Things ought to be different when Christians date. We're not like the world. We're not supposed to imitate the relational habits of unbelievers.

Take for example the whole issue of "flirting and signals." What do most people do? The list is almost endless. They wink, stare with bedroom eyes, smile, tease playfully, write cutsey notes, send mysterious e-mail, leave ambiguous phone messages, speak in code.

Scott Adams, creator of the wildly funny comic strip "Dilbert" captures the game well:

Dilbert: There … I've plotted Jenny Dworkin's normal speed, habits, and tendencies into my computer. Now I'll be able to predict her location and bump into her as if by chance.

Dogbert: Why don't you just call her, say you like her, and ask her out?

Dilbert: No. That would seem too contrived.

While it's clearly fun and intriguing to "play the game" of sending, receiving, and trying to interpret nonverbal signals, here's a vote for being more direct and upfront.

If you're interested in getting to know someone, don't beat around the bush! Stop resorting to dipping her ponytail in the inkwell, dropping your books in front of his locker, or having a friend call for you! Make direct contact.

A note to women: You may think that this is old-fashioned or sexist or an unfair double standard, but there are still quite a number of men who will be "turned off" if you are *too* aggressive. Many theologians and respected Bible teachers point out that God designed men to initiate and women to respond, and they argue that this is seen even in the physical differences between the sexes. For women, the difficulty with being more passive in dating is resisting the temptation to try to make something happen.

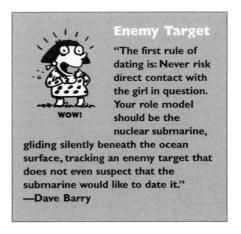

Enemy Target

"The first rule of dating is: Never risk direct contact with the girl in question. Your role model should be the nuclear submarine, gliding silently beneath the ocean surface, tracking an enemy target that does not even suspect that the submarine would like to date it."
—Dave Barry

WOW!

A note to men: By definition, masculinity means being willing to be bold, to initiate, to move into uncomfortable situations. It is NOT a healthy dynamic for a man to always sit back and wait for a woman to set the pace relationally. For men, the difficulty with taking the initiative in dating is risking rejection. Being turned down is enormously painful, but it is still preferable to developing a passive approach to male-female relationships.

HARD TO GET

CHASING A CAR

Playing "hard to get" is another game common in the world of dating. Someone has likened it to the phenomenon of a dog chasing a car. The whole thrill is the chase. The only reason the dog is motivated is because the car is moving. As soon as the vehicle stops, the dog is mystified about what to do, and the game is over.

Some play "hard to get" out of fear. A girl (usually) suspects that if she's "too available," a guy will lose interest. Or she might reason that if a guy gets to know the "real" her, he'll be grossed out, and end up dumping her and breaking her heart. So, she strings him along, teasing him with the tantalizing prospect of relationship, but never really allowing him to catch and know her.

THE DIFFERENCE BETWEEN "HARD TO GET" AND "NOT INTERESTED!"

Dilbert (peeking into a cubicle at work): Hi, Cheryl. Would you like to have lunch with me next week?

Cheryl: I … uh … already ate lunch. I'm not hungry.

Dilbert: I'm talking about *next week*!!

Cheryl (holding her stomach): I don't think I could have another bite. All full.

GUESSING GAME

WRONG GUESS

If you have an active imagination, the "guessing game" can keep you awake (usually nervous) for hours, even days after a date.

This is the game in which you play the roles of amateur psychologist, conversation decoder, and relational detective all at once. You take all the data (what was said, what was done, what was *not* said or done), and then you attempt to "read between the lines" to interpret the secret meaning of it all.

The problem with guessing is that we generally guess wrong. It's not hard to see why. First, we don't always have all the facts or even get straight the ones we *do* manage to collect. (It's very possible you misheard her comment or totally missed an important nonverbal signal). Second, nobody interprets facts accurately all the time. (Did you ever stop to think his grouchiness actually may have been due to the fact that he played the worst golf round of his life and is in no way related to the fact that you were having a "bad hair" day?) Third, trying to weave all these cryptic clues into a prediction about the future is like playing the lottery. ("There's no way he'll ever call/she'll ever go out with me again!") You don't know that! To agonize over things that only "might be" is to waste your time.

A big part of relational maturity is learning to listen and observe. Stop focusing on yourself and how you're coming across. Instead, take a genuine interest in the other person. Be honest and open and authentic. Ask questions. Jim Elliott once advised, "Wherever you are, be all there." That's great counsel for someone on a date. Engage fully. Enjoy your time together. Let God worry about the future, about what might (or might not) happen next.

Another healthy sign of growth is learning to take people at their word and accepting situations at face value. The "guessing game" can degenerate into paranoia and suspicion, if you start trying to find some hidden meaning in every glance or every comment. Fear over the future robs you of joy in the present! Why spend precious time and emotional energy obsessing over things beyond your control? Instead of wondering, fretting, worrying, and guessing (which all involve a nebulous future which only God knows), live in the present.

Ultimately it comes down to whether we believe God is good, whether we trust that He has a wise plan and that He will direct us in ways that are best for us.

Your date *may* have taken you home early because he wasn't having fun, but he also may have cut the date short for the very reason he stated: Because he ate too much pizza and was about to hurl on your sofa.

MAKE HIM/HER JEALOUS

UNWISE MOVE

It's not hard to make a potential date jealous. If it's obvious they're interested, all you have to do is something like:

- Drool and gush nonstop over the hunky leading man in the movie you're watching.
- Plaster posters of gorgeous, bikini-clad women all over your apartment.
- Give yourself whiplash doing doubletakes and gawking at every attractive person who passes you at the mall.
- Let her catch you with a supermodel, making out on the couch.
- Talk incessantly about all the other cute and sweet guys who have been asking you out lately.

The bigger questions are "Should a Christian resort to trying to induce jealousy?" and "Why would you even try to make someone jealous?"

Should a Christian Resort to Trying to Induce Jealousy? Consider that the New Testament contains some 30 different commands about how Christians are supposed to treat "one another" (e.g., "love another another," John 13:34; "accept one another," Romans 15:7; "serve one another," Galatians 5:13 etc.).

You'll never find a single instance where God tells his people, "Make one another jealous." However, there *are* numerous references that frown upon jealousy. Furthermore, 1 Thessalonians 5:11 exhorts us to "encourage one another" and Hebrews 10:24 calls us to "consider how we may spur one another on toward love and good deeds."

Why Would You Even Try to Make Someone Jealous? Such an attempt is always driven by insecurity. You want to feel desirable. What better way (so it seems) than to create a situation in which you know the object of your affection is practically going mad, worrying about losing you? The jealousy game, then, is purely selfish. In your desire to feel wanted, you are willing to put someone else through an emotional ringer.

This is an ideal place to inject the "Golden Rule" (Matthew 7:12). *You* would hate to be treated in such a fashion. So don't dare do it to others!

WHAT'S MY LINE? (PICK UP LINES)

DO THEY EVER WORK?

Through the ages, men (mostly) have tried to hit on women by using what are commonly known as "pick up" lines. It's been this way ever since the caveman Grak saw an attractive female named Blug down at the bog, and inquired, "Come here often?"

HERE ARE SOME OPENING LINES THAT ARE EMBARRASSINGLY STUPID

- Could I have your phone number? I lost mine.
- In rural areas: Wow! You're prettier than a speckled pup under a wheelbarrow!
- Can you keep a secret? I'm really Brad Pitt. I just put on this ugly, lifelike, rubber mask so that I could escape all the other girls in my quest to meet you.
- I've been watching you all evening. I'm dying to know … are you on (Rogaine, Weight Watchers, SlimFast—take your pick)?
- At the carwash: I'll wash your bumper if you'll wash mine.
- At a restaurant: I'll bet their apple pie isn't nearly as sweet as you are.
- I like to play the field, but I think I just hit a homerun with you.
- Thanks to Mulder and Scully, I have conclusive evidence that we were sweethearts in a prior life.
- My uncle Bill (Gates, that is) has given me a month to find a girl and settle down. Otherwise, he says I can forget that one billion dollars he promised.

Whew! There are better ways to meet folks. How about these simple, straightforward "opening lines"?

- Hi. I'm _____. What's your name?
- I know this is pretty forward, but I really wanted to come up and meet you.
- It took a lot of nerve for me to approach you, so can I at least ask your name?
- Can I buy you lunch?
- You look like you could use some help.
- I'm new at this. Can you help me out?
- I'm curious. What do *you* think about this place?

LEADING SOMEONE ON

NOT INTERESTED?

It's a sad thing, but sooner or later almost everyone encounters a situation in which they are being pursued by someone they are clearly *not* interested in. There can be a million and one reasons for such a mismatch, but the issue we want to look at now is: How does a person gracefully extricate himself/herself from such a situation?

Our exhaustive scientific research (i.e., yelling a question or two to several colleagues working in other cubicles here in the office) indicates that more than 99 percent of noninstitutionalized people would prefer to know the truth (even if it's painful). Better to know *now* that the relationship has no future, than down the road when the heart is even more vulnerable. Think about it … do you know a single person who *wants* to be "led on"? Do you?

WHAT TO DO IF YOU SENSE YOU'RE LOSING INTEREST

1. *Pray*. Ask God to help you distinguish between normal moodiness and a genuine loss of interest.
2. *Get counsel*. Don't go in a chat room on the Net, but discreetly pull aside an older, wiser friend. Verbalize what's taking place. Solicit his/her prayer.
3. *Think*. Spend time analyzing the relationship and especially your own heart. What's going on in you to make you reluctant to commit to this

relationship? Is it her passion for Hungarian folk dancing? Or are you pulling back due to fear? Is this is a pattern in your life?

4. *Decide*. Either move forward with the relationship or graciously (and gracefully) exit. Don't leave someone hanging while you go back and forth in your mind for weeks and weeks. Sometimes in our desire NOT to hurt others, we end up stringing them along and hurting them even more!

5. *Communicate truthfully and tenderly*. Ephesians 4:15 tells us to speak the truth in love. Nothing less than that is required here. It may be that your own emotional baggage is impeding the relationship. If so, say so. Let it be clear that the problem is with you. On the other hand, if the obstacle in the relationship is a deficiency in the other person (e.g., he's overbearing), be extremely careful what you say and how you say it.

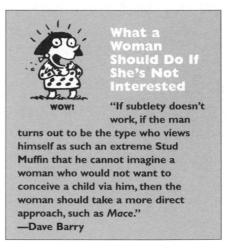

WOW!

What a Woman Should Do If She's Not Interested

"If subtlety doesn't work, if the man turns out to be the type who views himself as such an extreme Stud Muffin that he cannot imagine a woman who would not want to conceive a child via him, then the woman should take a more direct approach, such as *Mace*."
—**Dave Barry**

DATING SOMEONE ELSE BEHIND YOUR DATE'S BACK

IS ALL FAIR?

They say all is fair in love and war. But generally speaking, the only ones who say this are the ones who aren't bleeding to death (emotionally or physically)!

The issue before us is *dating more than one person at a time*. Is it right? Should *you*?

It all depends on your definition of "dating."

If you're a "free agent," that is, you have no commitments to anyone, no stated or unstated understandings, you're just dating around, playing the field … then it's acceptable to go out with one person one night and another individual the next. (Be forewarned, however, that if you enjoy this kind of social life, you will be tagged as a "player," "a womanizer," "a flirt," or worse. Such labels generally come from those who are jealous of your dating success.)

If, however, you are *dating* someone (by that we mean you have had the infamous DTR Discussion*, in which you've made it clear that you are mutually interested in getting to know each other better and taking the next step toward couplehood), then to go out with others is flat wrong. Do this, and you are worthy of any bad name others might throw at you!

Historical footnote: It used to be that people who "double-dipped" in the realm of dating were shunned by the larger group. An unwritten code of honor meant that whole sororities would blacklist a guy who was discovered dating other girls behind his girlfriend's (and their sister's) back. Similarly, groups of males would mutually agree to ignore or avoid, and thereby punish, a female who committed this unpardonable sin.

Nowadays, this behavior is not only accepted, it's proudly practiced. People who get really good at it often move to Hollywood where their conniving ways are glamorized on shows like *Melrose Place* and *The Young and the Selfish*.

*A "Define The Relationship" chat

SECTION 14

....

SAFETY TIPS

GETTING OUT

A GUT FEELING

Sue scratched her head. She couldn't understand Alan's last e-mail message. He seemed pushy somehow. She couldn't help feeling ... uncomfortable.

Have you ever experienced this feeling? Getting involved in a relationship can be fun. But sometimes, in a person's quest for companionship, he or she fails to heed the call of caution. You know the sign: that uncomfortable feeling you get when someone attempts to rush you into something you may not be ready for, or to cross a line you shouldn't cross.

Free Advice

THE BIBLE SAYS

God promises to direct his people and watch over them. (See Psalm 32:8; Proverbs 3:5–6.) **One way He directs us is through the wisdom he offers.**

If you experience this, give yourself time to prayerfully examine the reason behind the feeling. God does not want His people to walk in fear or paranoia. He does, however, want His people to be wise. Is the nervousness really fear? Was there something a person said or did that challenged you beyond your comfort zone? If the latter was the case, make sure you seek clarification from the person before going further in the relationship. If, however, you feel afraid, always err on the side of caution. When in doubt, get out!

How Do You Get Out of a Situation That Makes You Uncomfortable?

Move slowly. Evaluate what's being asked of you. If someone is trying to rush you into a relationship, and you're not ready for one, don't allow yourself to be talked into it. Instead, be honest. "I'm not ready for a relationship right now." If you'd still like to get to know the person, explain that you'd like to move slowly. On the flip side, if you're keeping someone hanging because you can't make up your mind about a relationship, cut the string. Own up to the indecision. If you can't make up your mind, don't keep someone else waiting.

Move wisely. If you've met someone on the Internet or through a personal ad, do not agree to a face-to-face meeting until you feel "safer." You might feel safe if you know more about the person. Until that happens, monitor the amount of personal information you disclose. A person might make you feel nervous if he or she asks you to disclose too much information too quickly or tells you too much about herself at the first instance of meeting. You don't have to share information you don't feel comfortable sharing. For example, if you don't want to give out your phone number, don't give it.

If someone you meet on the Internet makes you uncomfortable, break off contact. If the person persists to the point of harassing you, report him/her to the appropriate authorities. Your Internet carrier has more details about reporting online nuisances. You'll need to explain the exact nature of the harassment. For example, if the person is being obscene or threatening, here is one web site to remember: http://www.fbi.gov (the FBI's web site).

Move away. If someone you're talking to in a public place makes you feel nervous, avoid giving out essentials like a phone number and address. Instead, conclude the conversation and move away from that person. Gauge your surroundings, then move toward the center of a crowd, toward a friend if he or she is nearby, or toward an area]with more light. If a security guard is nearby, move toward him, but only if the person seems threatening or persists in annoying you. If you do feel threatened by this individual, do not head toward the exit until you're certain that the person is not attempting to follow you. If you're still nervous about being followed to your car or dorm room, ask a guard or campus security to walk you to your car or get a friend to go with you.

DO YOU TRUST ME?

(AN YOU TRUST YET?

Trust. According to the *American Heritage Dictionary,* trust is "firm reliance on the integrity, ability, or character of a person or thing." Do you know your date well enough to trust him/her? The questions below can help you decide.

1. I've known him or her
> A. for less than a week.
> B. between one to three months.
> C. between six months to a year.
> D. for over a year.

2. I know that he or she
> A. is definitely a strong Christian.
> B. is definitely a new Christian.
> C. *might* be a Christian.
> D. is definitely not a Christian.

3. In the time that I have known him or her, he or she
> A. has never lied to me.
> B. has lied to me once or twice.
> C. has lied to me more than three times.
> D. has consistently lied to me.

4. My friends/family members say that he or she
> A. is definitely not what he or she seems.
> B. seems nice.
> C. is not to be trusted.
> D. A and C

5. My heart tells me
> A. I can trust him or her.
> B. I definitely cannot trust him or her.
> C. I should be cautious.
> D. I need to know more about him or her.
> E. C and D

6. In the last week, he or she
> A. surprised me by an act of kindness.
> B. surprised me by an act of cruelty.
> C. behaved consistently with what I know about his/her character.
> D. seemed consistently inconsistent.

7. Overall, I'd say that he or she
> A. is consistent in his or her character.
> B. is inconsistent in his or her character.
> C. is a complete enigma.
> D. B and C

Question one: Trust builds the more you know about a person. The shorter the amount of time you've known a person, the least likely it is for trust to have built up. In rare instances, you might meet a person you instinctively know that you can trust.

Question two: A person can profess to be a Christian but may not necessarily be trustworthy, particularly if you don't see evidence in their character (see Matthew 7:17–20 and Galatians 5:22–23).

Question three: A person who lies to you diminishes in trustworthiness with every lie. A person who consistently lies to you cannot be trusted. If the person who lied to you is willing to repent, he or she will need to earn your trust once more.

Question four: Watch what friends or family members say, especially if you know they have a godly perspective. No matter how attractive and wonderful a person may seem, if a friend tells you that your date is not all that he/she seems, take that seriously.

Question five: The heart can sometimes lead us into trouble (see Jeremiah 17:9), but it can also warn us when something isn't right.

Question six: Surprising acts of behavior can reveal a lot about a person, whether good or bad. Only time will tell if the behavior is consistent with what you know about the person. A cruel act, even if the person cites stress as an excuse, will always be a mark against a person's trustworthiness.

Question seven: Consistency of character lets you know a person is trustworthy. As you get to know a person, you can observe whether he or she is consistent.

The following are more questions you can ask yourself. If the answers are consistently negative, trusting the person might not be the wisest course.

- Has the person ever told someone something you told him or her in confidence?
- Has the person been pleased or reluctant to reveal details about himself or herself?
- Is the person usually where he or she says he/she will be whenever you try to contact him/her?
- Has the person's friends or family members revealed details about the person that seem consistent or inconsistent with what you know about him/her?

DON'T GO THERE!

OUT OF HARM'S WAY?

There are also some places that look safe, but are really dangerous. A date might be fun, but use your common sense. There's no need to take risks with your physical safety or the safety of your date.

COMMON SENSE PLACES TO AVOID WHILE ON A DATE

- forest preserves at night
- dark alleys (it's better to go the long way, please, no shortcuts)
- strange neighborhoods
- swimming or diving at a waterfront that you are not familiar with without a lifeguard on duty
- running or biking on secluded paths at night
- no trespassing areas
- anything marked private property
- unlocked parked cars
- empty, unlit parking lots
- the outdoors during a storm
- parties with drugs or alcohol
- large concerts that are likely to get violent
- walks near train tracks
- driving when road conditions are poor

MONEY MATTERS

MONEY SAFETY

You've seen those Visa™ commercials where a grinning clerk fawns over a celebrity who is making a purchase, right? After all of the fawning, the clerk finally stops grinning and demands to see some ID. He or she doesn't want to be taken advantage of, even by a celebrity.

The sad fact about living in a fallen world is that some people do try to take advantage of others. More than likely you've read about con artists who tricked unsuspecting individuals into giving them thousands of dollars. These clever individuals either had an abundance of charm or a "sad sack" story they used to gain the trust of someone.

You owe it to yourself to make sure you're protected financially.

WAYS TO INSURE YOUR FINANCIAL SAFETY

Don't share your credit card information. This is information no one needs to know, unless you're ordering something from a catalog. Don't allow anyone to use your credit card.

Don't discuss your bank account information. Again, this is information no one but you is entitled to know. If you're ill and need a trusted (accent on *trusted*) individual to make a bank deposit for you, that's a different matter. But a boyfriend or girlfriend does not need to know.

Be cautious about giving money. Many Christians have fallen prey to individuals who take advantage of their generous natures. Although the Bible does tell us to share with one another (Matthew 6:3–4; 2 Corinthians 9:6–15), it also tells us to be wise (Matthew 10:16). Giving a few dollars is one thing. Giving a large sum of money is another. Do not give money to an individual you don't know well until you can investigate the need. Instead, you might recommend an agency (an on-campus group; a Christian relief organization; a church) who can help him or her, or find someone trustworthy who can vouch for that person. If the person you date is poor, his or her need will be apparent to you.

Be cautious about giving expensive gifts. Expensive gifts usually raise red flags, especially if you're just getting to know a person. God wants His people to be good stewards of their resources. Money is a resource. Examine your reason for giving the person an expensive gift. Realize that an expensive gift is not a substitute for love, nor will it cause a person to love you. If you sense that a boyfriend or girlfriend expects expensive gifts in order to remain in a relationship with you, grab your Visa™ and run—don't walk—to the nearest exit.

OKAY, I'VE BEEN DUPED. NOW WHAT?

If you've fallen prey to someone who has taken advantage of you financially:

Don't allow shame to keep you from telling someone. It's natural to feel embarrassed, but don't keep this to yourself. Instead, tell someone: your bank, a friend, the police or the local branch of the FBI. The police can help you get in touch with the FBI if you're uncertain. If you're online, however, go to the FBI's web page (http://www.fbi.gov). You'll find local listings for the FBI under the section "Your FBI." Con artists count on a victim's shame to cloak their movements. Many are able to get away with what they've done because they know the individual is too embarrassed or afraid to report the crime. Ask God for the courage to do what needs to be done. Your actions may prevent another person from becoming a victim.

Learn from your mistakes or the mistakes of others. No one likes to learn the hard way, yet mistakes can sometimes be our best teachers. "Whoever gives heed to instruction prospers, and blessed is he who trusts in the LORD" (Proverbs 16:20). Don't beat yourself up over this mistake nor "fret because of evil men" or "when [men] carry out their wicked schemes" (Psalm 37:1, 7). Ask God to fill your heart with the hope of His love and the knowledge that He is in control.

WARNING!

WARNING SIGNS

He refuses to disclose his home phone number. A home phone number helps establish a person's identity. Although you're wise not to hand out your home phone number *right away* to a person you just met through a personal ad or through the Internet, eventually you should know whether or not you can trust the person with the information. If the person still insists on being contacted only through a beeper number or work number, you might find that he or she is married or hiding something else.

She comes on too fast. Someone who is intent to sweep you off your feet as quickly as possible might have an agenda she is not disclosing.

He hardly reveals any facts about himself. If you've known this person for a while and realize you still know very little about him, he may be trouble or *in* trouble.

She seems too good to be true. Someone who *seems* overly sweet, charming, or thoughtful probably isn't. Ask God's help for discernment to tell what's real from what's false. If someone is *genuinely* loving, you won't have to question her motives. The fruit of the Spirit will be evident. (See Galatians 5:22-23; see also Acts 6:3; 1 Peter 3:4.)

He seems possessive, jealous, or controlling. A person who genuinely wants to know you will want to know things about you: who you are, who your friends are, what you do, and so on. This information is gradually given as you get to know each other and trust is built up. A jealous or possessive person might be overly concerned about who your friends are, particularly friends of the opposite sex and past relationships. One of the signs of this is someone who keeps asking you about a current friend or an old boyfriend/girlfriend and whether you're interested in that person. He or she also might greet anyone you meet or mention with suspicion. A controlling person might expect you to account for your movements at all times and demand to have input in every decision you make, even at the beginning stages of getting to know you.

If you've made a commitment to a person, that person does have some input into your life. He or she also expects certain commitment behaviors from you, including a reassurance that you're *committed* to that commitment. If the person you're with demands this reassurance time and time again, and you know you've behaved in a way that proves your commitment, you may have a problem on your hands.

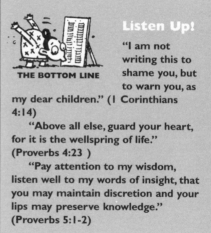

THE BOTTOM LINE

Listen Up!

"I am not writing this to shame you, but to warn you, as my dear children." (I Corinthians 4:14)

"Above all else, guard your heart, for it is the wellspring of life." (Proverbs 4:23)

"Pay attention to my wisdom, listen well to my words of insight, that you may maintain discretion and your lips may preserve knowledge." (Proverbs 5:1-2)

She seems obsessive. The person calls five or six times a day, wants to be with you every moment, follows you around, and won't take no for an answer when you say you cannot go out with her. All she wants to talk about is how the two of you belong together. If the behavior persists, even after you confront the person and attempt to break off communication, you may have a stalker on your hands. Stalkers act upon their obsessions. If you find this is the case, don't give in to the person to make the problem go away. Instead, get help.

SECTION 15

THE COURTSHIP ALTERNATIVE

COURTSHIP

WHAT IS IT?

Recently many Christians have decided to dump dating. They're tired of it or think it's too risky. They're not interested in breaking their own hearts or the hearts of others. As a result, they've chosen an alternative—*No, not mail-order brides!*—they've decided to court rather than date.

Some people call it courtship. Some call it biblical dating. Some even call it betrothal. And everyone who calls it any of those things means something slightly different by it. So, how do you explain what courtship—or any of those other names for it—is? In the words of the great Inigo Montoya of *The Princess Bride*, "Let me explain. No, it's too much. Let me sum up...."

WHY THE ALTERNATIVE TO DATING?

Sean and Sylvia

Sean thought Sylvia was perfect when they first started dating. She was pretty, athletic, and smart. What more could you want in a girl? Well, after a few months, he found out. He learned the hard way that he also wanted someone who shared his views on what's right and wrong, someone who didn't think cheating on a test or lying to your parents was alright. He learned he wanted someone who used God's name as more than part of a swear word. And he learned he wanted someone who wouldn't start going out with another guy behind his back. Yeah, he learned a lot alright. And he's not sure he wants to do any more of that kind of learning ever again.

Ashley and Zac

Ashley and Zac met at a football game when she was a sophomore and he was a junior. A mutual friend introduced them, and they hit it off right away.

He called her the next day and asked her out. The rest was history, so to speak. He walked her to class, even carrying her books, and she wrote him sweet little notes and stuck them in his locker. Their friends gagged over the pet names they called each other, things like "muffin lips" and "shnookie-wookums" and "honey-buggy-boogie-bear." They talked on the phone every night and went out almost every weekend.

During the summer, they got jobs working at the same store and spent their days off at the beach together. They went to every dance together, including Homecoming and, eventually, Zac's senior prom. At Zac's graduation, Ashley was the proud, smiling, supportive girlfriend. Then, fall came and Zac got ready to go to college. He promised Ashley that nothing would change. They could still talk on the phone, and he'd try to come home most weekends so they could be together—after all, it was only a five-hour drive. Believing in her heart that Zac was "the one," Ashley believed that everything would work out. Zac said he loved her, and true love always won in the end, right?

That first semester was hard, but they tried to make it work. They still talked almost every day, and Zac made it home at least every other weekend. Christmas break was a dream-come-true for both of them. But the next semester, Zac decided on a premed major and started taking some really hard classes. He had to spend extra time in the labs and started studying late at the library. He'd forget to call Ashley, and when she called him, he wasn't home. Zac started making new friends, one of whom talked him into joining a group that went into the inner city and tutored kids in some of the poorer neighborhoods. That meant his weekends weren't always free, and when they were, he had to spend more time catching up on homework. He started going home less and less.

After a couple months, Ashley confronted him on the phone. She hadn't wanted to say anything before because the things he was doing were all good things, but where did that leave her? Zac didn't think he should give up any of the things that kept him from Ashley. And he didn't think Ashley should stay at home waiting for him, either. So, he said, even though he loved her, maybe it was time for them to break up. Their lives were going in different directions, and maybe they shouldn't fight it. Ashley hung up the phone sobbing. So this was what it felt like to have a broken heart. This wasn't the way it was supposed to be. They were going to live happily ever after, like in the movies. They'd promised each other. Ashley wasn't sure she ever wanted to open herself up to that kind of hurt again!

Kendra

The youngest of five girls, Kendra watched her four older sisters hit the dating scene. She saw them pair up with different guys, then saw them break up. She noticed how people in their youth group tended to "choose sides" after those break ups, and the division that caused in the group. One guy broke up with her sister, saying, "I'd really rather just be friends." But Kendra noticed that he and her sister were never really friends after that; it was just too hard after she'd given her heart to him and had it broken. She saw how one of her other sisters put all her time and energy into her boyfriend, and how when they broke up, she didn't have any close friends anymore. Another sister gave up following her dream of studying marine biology in Hawaii so she could go to school closer to her boyfriend. After a semester together at the community college, he told her he was interested in someone else. Kendra started thinking to herself, *If that's what dating is, then I'm not sure it's for me. There's got to be a better way!*

REASONS FOR THE ALTERNATIVE

Let's start with looking at some of the reasons why anyone would want or need to find an alternative to dating.

Dating can lead to intimacy but not always commitment. It awakens desires, both emotional and physical, that neither person is really ready or able to meet. You long to be close in ways that only married people should be. So you either give in to temptation or experience great frustration until you do marry each other—or you undergo the heartache that comes from breaking up with someone who you've given parts of yourself to either physically or emotionally. Dating encourages emotional attachment without the protection of a promise, at least not a promise that both people are always able to keep.

Dating tends to skip the "friendship" stage of a relationship. Usually people date because they're attracted to each other and want to get to know each other, right? They jump right past the friendship stage and tend to focus on the attraction that brought them together, not common interests or other things that they might share. What "commitment" there is between them is shallow because it's based on feelings, which are prone to change. When the attraction passes and the romance fades, the relationship's over. Intimacy without friendship is superficial and won't last.

Dating often mistakes a physical relationship for real love. You think that because you feel all warm and fuzzy when you holds hands or when he kisses you that this must be love, and the "real thing" at that, or else why would you feel this way? God created us to enjoy physical affection, but that doesn't mean it's love. It could just as well be lust.

Dating tends to isolate a couple from other important relationships. We've all seen it happen. Two people start dating and suddenly all their other friendships fall by the wayside. They focus all their time and energy on each other and don't invest much into their relationships with family and friends.

And what happens when they break up? At best, they find themselves having to play catch-up and having missed out on a lot with those people. At worst, they find that they no longer have any friends and they're out of touch with their family. And was it really worth it?

Dating can distract young people from preparing for their future. High school and college are crucial periods in the life of a young man or woman as they develop skills and explore opportunities which will determine the course of their future. It takes time to do that. And sometimes people who are dating use up all their time and energy maintaining their relationship, leaving little left over to prepare for the future. Dating can also distract you from serving God and developing your relationship with Him, which is the most important thing you could do to prepare for the future.

Dating can cause discontentment with singleness. God says it's good to be single, and singleness is certainly not the end of the world. In fact, single people don't have the distraction of pleasing and caring for another person and can serve God in ways that married people can't. Dating can give single people just enough intimacy to want more and make them unhappy about being single. They're so busy not wanting to be single that they miss out on the good things about being single.

Dating can create an artificial atmosphere for evaluating another person's character. If you want to really get to know a person, dating may not be the best way to do it. On a date, you tend to "put your best foot forward." Few people go out to dinner and let their date see how they have a quick temper, or how they like to have their own way, or how selfish they are. If their date sees those things, it's not because they wanted them to, that's for sure! Instead, they want their date to see how patient they are, how flexible they can be, and how loving and giving—and they'll work hard at saying and doing things to demonstrate that. And that's pretty easy to do when you only spend a few hours with someone. If you really want to get to know someone, you're better off doing it in group settings than on a date. In a group, you can watch them without their knowing it. And when you see them with their family, then you're really going to get the real "them." You need to see each other in the real-life settings of working and serving with family and friends and acquaintances if you want to know one another.

Dating doesn't train you to form a relationship, but a series of relationships. It also trains you to harden yourself to break ups—accepting them as normal and natural. What kind of preparation is this for marriage? Not very good if you want to have a marriage that is committed to one person for the rest of your life.

Dating tends to leave the father of the girl out of the picture. The Bible teaches that fathers have an important role in the daughter's life. She is to be given in marriage under his authority and guidance, which is something that recreational dating as we know it doesn't tend to promote.

THE ULTIMATE GOAL

Okay, so if you're looking for an alternative, what alternative is there? That's where courtship comes in.

Let's start with looking at the goal of dating versus the goal of courtship. Dating usually involves two people spending time alone together because they're attracted to each other and they think it would be fun. Dating can start as young as junior high, and most people have begun dating at least by the time they enter college.

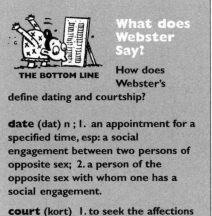

THE BOTTOM LINE

What does Webster Say?

How does Webster's define dating and courtship?

date (dat) n ; 1. an appointment for a specified time, esp: a social engagement between two persons of opposite sex; 2. a person of the opposite sex with whom one has a social engagement.

court (kort) 1. to seek the affections of, esp: to seek to win a pledge of marriage from; 2. to engage in social activities leading to engagement and marriage.

Depending on each person, the goal of dating might be different, but the most common goals are: having a good time, finding romance, getting to know someone, and so forth.

Courtship looks at things from a different perspective. It's more serious than dating in that the goal of courtship is marriage, so you don't begin courting until you're ready to get married. Two people who have already gotten to know each other through church or other group settings believe that they might be interested in marrying

What's the Best Way to Prepare for Marriage?

WIDE ANGLE

• Develop a heart that loves God more and more.
• **Learn to deny yourself and put aside your own needs to meet those of others.**
• **Look for opportunities to love others, even when it's not easy.**
• **Ask God to develop your character and show you areas to work on.**

each other. So, they get to know each other better by spending time with each other's families. The decision on whether or not they then get engaged and married is not left to the couple alone, but also to their parents, especially the girl's father.

WHAT IS MARRIAGE?

If marriage is the goal of courtship, then it's important to understand that goal.

It was the first institution which God ordained—even before the family, the church, or government.

It's meant to be a life-long covenant between a man and woman whom God brings together to work as a team for His glory.

It's a living picture of the relationship between Jesus Christ and the Church. It's meant to demonstrate the sacrificial love of Christ, and the loving submission and respect of the Church. (You can look at Ephesians 5 for more on this.)

It's a union which God wants us to honor, to value as precious, and to view with respect and awe.

WHAT SHOULD YOU LOOK FOR IN A MARRIAGE PARTNER?

Use this worksheet to evaluate whether or not the person you're interested in courting would make a good spouse for you.

1. Is he or she a Christian? Does he/she feel the same way that you do about God and your relationship with Him? How is that evidenced in his/her life?

2. Are you like-minded about your faith? Do you have the same doctrinal perspectives? (For example, do you share the same views on what salvation means, on the importance of baptism, God's role in the world today, etc.)

3. If you're a girl, is the guy ready financially to support a family? Does he demonstrate financial stability and responsibility? How do you know this?

What is his attitude toward money and material things? How does this match up with your own attitude?

4. How does he/she respond to authority figures such as parents, pastors, employers, and government?

5. How does he/she treat members of the opposite sex? Does she flirt? Does he open doors for all girls, or just for you—the one he's trying to impress? Does he/she display respect and integrity in their relationships with others? Do you?

6. Who are his/her closest friends? What three adjectives would best describe those friends? What can you learn about your potential spouse from his/her choice in friends?

7. If you're a guy, how does your potential wife dress? Does she take care with her appearance, but without being flashy or preoccupied with it? Or is she overly engrossed in her clothes and makeup? Is her appearance characterized by modesty?

8. How does he/she approach their work responsibilities? Does he give it his all and work hard to do his very best, or is he content to just get by with expending the minimum amount of energy necessary to squeak by in fulfilling the requirements? How does that compare with your approach?

9. How would you describe his/her general attitude about life? Does she usually see the glass as half-full or half-empty? Is he generally content, or is he more likely to be complaining about something? Does she see life as an adventure to be shared, or as a trial to be endured? How does that compare with your own attitude?

10. Do you respect each other? How do you know? What evidence is there to prove it?

FAMILY FIRST

COURTING EMPHASIZES FAMILY

In dating, the couple's family may or may not be involved. Usually, the girl's parents will want to meet the guy before they go out, and they might spend time at each other's houses. But the role of the family is usually minimal instead of foundational.

In courtship, there is a huge emphasis on family. When a guy sees a girl he's interested in perhaps marrying, he begins by speaking with the girl's parents about it. If they think he might make a good husband for their daughter, and if their daughter is interested also, then the courting begins. This involves primarily spending time with one another's families. This is where the couple really gets to know each other. It's

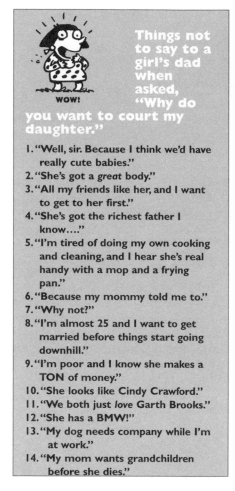

WOW!

Things not to say to a girl's dad when asked, "Why do you want to court my daughter."

1. "Well, sir. Because I think we'd have really cute babies."
2. "She's got a *great* body."
3. "All my friends like her, and I want to get to her first."
4. "She's got the richest father I know…."
5. "I'm tired of doing my own cooking and cleaning, and I hear she's real handy with a mop and a frying pan."
6. "Because my mommy told me to."
7. "Why not?"
8. "I'm almost 25 and I want to get married before things start going downhill."
9. "I'm poor and I know she makes a TON of money."
10. "She looks like Cindy Crawford."
11. "We both just *love* Garth Brooks."
12. "She has a BMW!"
13. "My dog needs company while I'm at work."
14. "My mom wants grandchildren before she dies."

hard to put up a good front when you've got your little brother around to help point out the "other side." And you're not going to tell anything but the truth, and the whole truth, when your parents are sitting there at the dinner table with the two of you. You're bound to be honest and open when you've got your siblings there to tell about the time when you were five and you super glued your mouth shut, or about when you were ten and you fell asleep in church and fell off your chair into the aisle, or about when you were thirteen and you gave a speech in front of the whole school with the fly of your pants undone.... Your

CATCH A CLUE

Quote from I Kissed Dating Goodbye by Joshua Harris

"Just because something is good doesn't mean we should pursue it right now. We have to remember that the right thing at the wrong time is the wrong thing."

family has a way of bringing out all of who you are—both the good and the bad—which is what you need to find out about each other if you're going to decide to marry.

At this stage, parents are also involved in helping process through with their son or daughter their thoughts on what they are learning about each other and whether or not this person is indeed the one that God would have them marry. Parents help to provide encouragement and guidance, as well as accountability for emotional and physical purity in the relationship. And when it comes to where the couple is ready to take the steps of engagement and marriage, the family again plays a huge part as the couple looks to them for wisdom and advice and permission to move to the next phase in their relationship.

	DATING OVERVIEW	**COURTSHIP OVERVIEW**
How old are people when they start?	Varies—usually sometime during high school	When they are ready to get married—usually sometime after high school
How does it start?	Usually two people are romantically attracted to each other, and one asks the other to go out on a date	Two people have already gotten to know each other in group settings (church, work, volunteer ministries, etc.) and think the other person might make a good spouse. Romantic interest is usually there but is not the driving force.
How does a couple spend their time together?	Sometimes in group dates, and sometimes at each other's homes. Usually most of their time "dating" is spent alone together doing things like going to dinner, going on walks, seeing concerts or movies, etc.	A couple does their "courting" in group settings, basically by spending time with each other's families.
Role of parents and family	Lots of variety. Girl's parents may want to meet the guy before they go out, or they may not. Most parents like to casually get to know the person their son or daughter is seeing, and so may include them in family activities.	Critical to courtship. They oversee, watch, and help arrange the advancement of the relationship.
The goal	Varies. It can be simply having fun, growing close, or planning for marriage.	Marriage

THE BASICS OF THE ACTUAL PROCESS

OK, I WANT TO KISS DATING GOODBYE

Okay, so you're convinced. Courtship sounds like the right thing for you. You even think you might be ready to get started. Now you want to know, "Just what, exactly, do I do?"

It's difficult to give a specific, one-size-fits-all answer to that question. Just like every snowflake is different, every courtship will be different. At the same time, there are some basic elements that definitely make up every snowflake. And there are some basic steps that you should find in any courtship.

Step One: Getting the Family on Board
First, if it's your idea—as opposed to your parents'—to take the courtship approach, you need to sit down and have a long talk with them. Tell them what it is you want to do, and what you want them to do, and why. You may want to ask them to take a look at the suggested reading. This thing won't work if your parents are unwilling or don't understand the role that you'd like them to play. If your parents aren't Christians, or don't want to be that involved with the process, it may be a little harder, but you can still make it work. When you get to where you want to begin the actual "courting," you can still talk to your parents about it. If you're female, you can still ask the young man to speak to your parents first. You can then make it a point to spend time together at each other's homes, making sure that family members will be around. At the same time, you can look for someone else—an

older couple from church, perhaps—who would be willing to be "adoptive parents" in the courtship process. You can then also spend time as a couple at their home, asking them to hold you accountable and to evaluate your relationship. When the time comes to make a decision on whether to continue the relationship and become engaged, this couple can serve as a source of wisdom and encouragement in making the right choice. You don't remove your own parents from the picture, but you add another element to it. And if your parents are more than ready and willing to be involved in this with you, then you can be extra thankful for that!

Step Two: The Initial Getting to Know Someone
The best way to start getting to know someone is in group settings. Places like church, school, work, ministry settings, and various social gatherings all provide a forum for initially learning a lot about a person. It's easy to discern what type of personality they have—boisterous and outgoing, or quiet and thoughtful. You can learn a lot about how they treat people, all different kinds of people, just by watching. From conversations you often discover what things are important to someone—just listen to what they tend to talk about most. You can usually figure out what things a person is passionate about by where they choose to spend their time: If he's an usher and on the social committee, you can tell he likes people. If she's a Sunday school teacher, constantly baby-sitting, and seems to always be holding someone's baby, you can tell she likes children. If he's involved in prison ministries, takes home a pile of tracts from the back of the church each week, and is consistently asking prayer for the salvation of different non-Christians, you can tell he has a heart for evangelism. And so on, and so on. You get the idea. The bottom line is that you spend time building friendships and getting to know other people, lots of other people, in a variety of group settings.

Step Three: A Standout in the Crowd
You've enjoyed making friendships with many different people. You've

learned a lot about who they are and what makes them tick. And you think you may have found that "special someone." It seems like no matter what crowd they're in, he or she just can't help but stand out to you. You've assessed your own readiness to begin courtship, and feel the time has come. And you've taken the time to go through the "What You Should Look For in a Marriage Partner" worksheet, and this person came out looking like he or she might be the perfect spouse for you. But you want to find out more, get to know each other better, and find out if what you're thinking is actually right. Then what?

Step Four: Talking to the Parents

For a young woman, the next step is more "hands-off" than for a young man. If you've spotted someone who you think would make a good spouse for you, you should talk to your parents about it. Let them know what you're thinking and why, and ask them to pray with you and for you about the situation. Then—here's the hard part—you have to wait. It's up to him to make the first move, and if he's the guy God has for you, then he will.

    For a young man, the ball is pretty much in your court. Talk to your parents first about the young lady you're interested in. If they approve, then it's time to talk to the girl's parents. If her parents don't think you're the right person for their daughter, they may tell you right away. Or they may ask to get back to you. If they like you, they will probably talk to their daughter to see if she's also interested in getting to know you better. If the answer's yes, then they'll let you know that, and you can begin "courting."

Step Five: Spending Time Together

Especially initially, you'll be spending time together with each other's families, especially with the family of the young lady. This is a time not only for you as a couple to get to know each other but also for each other's families to get to know you. As your relationship grows more serious, the girl's father may give permission for you to spend time alone without the family—but most likely with certain restrictions and guidelines. You may be allowed to do such things as going out to dinner or to a concert, but not moonlit walks on the beach or drive-in movies. Here, the idea is protection and accountability—making sure that you're not in situations where you might be tempted to do more than you should or than would be wise at this time.

Step Six: Engagement?

If it becomes obvious to any of the parties involved—the young man or woman, or their parents—that these two would not make a suitable couple, then that should be discussed and the courtship ended before any commitment is made.

However, if it becomes apparent that this couple has been brought together by God, then engagement is definitely the next step. The young man should speak to the lady's parents and then to her. If, for some reason, the guy just doesn't seem to be taking any steps towards this—and a reasonable amount of time has passed—then the girl's father may want to have a little chat with the young man. It could be he just has cold feet about asking and needs a little encouragement. Or it could be that he's just not sure about the whole thing, and the father may need to send him on his way.

Once engaged, the couple can then begin really preparing for marriage—not only for the wedding but also for the lifetime together that comes after it. It's wise to be involved in some kind of premarital counseling through your church to further prepare you for what lies ahead. Remember that engagement—and the subsequent wedding—are not the end, they're just the beginning!

FREQUENTLY ASKED QUESTIONS

I've already dated a few different people. Is it too late to start courting?

No, definitely not. You can learn from these relationships and move on.

What if the guy I'm interested in wants to date—not court?

If he asks you out on a date, you should tell him that you and your family prefer an alternative to typical dating, and ask him to talk to your parents about it. If he's still interested, then your parents can explain courtship and they both can decide where to go from there. If he decides to blow you off because he doesn't want to do courtship, then God has someone else out there for you.

What if I like someone my parents don't approve of?

It's no mistake that you have your specific set of parents; God matched you up a long time ago. And your parents know you better than anyone else does. Add to that the fact that they're older and wiser than you. Top it off with the Bible's command to honor your father and mother, and you'll find that you'd better pay close attention to what your parents say. Even if they're wrong, God can work through their mistakes. Wait and pray, and see if God changes either their hearts or yours.

Is it possible to develop a close friendship if my parents are ALWAYS around?

It sure is. Unless you're someone who has a lot to hide from their parents and is not used to being open with them, you should be able to get to know each other quite well. Again, you may even find out things that you wouldn't find out if you just started out by spending your time alone together away from your families. And eventually, you will probably be spending some time together where your parents aren't around—at least not in the same room with you. But that will only happen after they feel comfortable with the idea of the two of you together.

Do I ever get a chance to be alone with this person?

Again, this will depend on the family, but chances are you will. But not until after you've really gotten to know each other and each other's families. And you'll probably be doing so under the watchful guidance of the girl's parents.

SUGGESTED READING:

I Kissed Dating Goodbye, by Joshua Harris
Her Hand in Marriage, by Douglas Wilson

INDEX